YOU WANT ME  S0-ASM-559

A guide to persuasive communication

PATRICK FORSYTH worked in publishing before moving into marketing consultancy and training. He is now head of his own company, Touchstone Training and Consultancy. His books include *Everything you need to know about marketing* (Kogan Page). Patrick Forsyth lives and works in Islington, London.

Overcoming Common Problems Series

Beating Job Burnout
DR DONALD SCOTT

Beating the Blues
SUSAN TANNER AND JILLIAN BALL

Being the Boss
STEPHEN FITZSIMON

Birth Over Thirty
SHEILA KITZINGER

Body Language
How to read others' thoughts by their gestures
ALLAN PEASE

Bodypower
DR VERNON COLEMAN

Bodysense
DR VERNON COLEMAN

Calm Down
How to cope with frustration and anger
DR PAUL HAUCK

Comfort for Depression
JANET HORWOOD

Common Childhood Illnesses
DR PATRICIA GILBERT

Complete Public Speaker
GYLES BRANDRETH

Coping Successfully with Your Child's Asthma
DR PAUL CARSON

Coping Successfully with Your Child's Skin Problems
DR PAUL CARSON

Coping Successfully with Your Hyperactive Child
DR PAUL CARSON

Coping Successfully with Your Irritable Bowel
ROSEMARY NICOL

Coping with Anxiety and Depression
SHIRLEY TRICKETT

Coping with Cot Death
SARAH MURPHY

Coping with Depression and Elation
DR PATRICK McKEON

Coping with Stress
DR GEORGIA WITKIN-LANOIL

Coping with Suicide
DR DONALD SCOTT

Coping with Thrush
CAROLINE CLAYTON

Curing Arthritis – The Drug-Free Way
MARGARET HILLS

Curing Arthritis Diet Book
MARGARET HILLS

Curing Coughs, Colds and Flu – The Drug-Free Way
MARGARET HILLS

Curing Illness – The Drug-Free Way
MARGARET HILLS

Depression
DR PAUL HAUCK

Divorce and Separation
ANGELA WILLANS

The Dr Moerman Cancer Diet
RUTH JOCHEMS

The Epilepsy Handbook
SHELAGH McGOVERN

Everything You Need to Know about Adoption
MAGGIE JONES

Everything You Need to Know about Contact Lenses
DR ROBERT YOUNGSON

Everything You Need to Know about Osteoporosis
ROSEMARY NICOL

Everything You Need to Know about Shingles
DR ROBERT YOUNGSON

Everything You Need to Know about Your Eyes
DR ROBERT YOUNGSON

Family First Aid and Emergency Handbook
DR ANDREW STANWAY

Overcoming Common Problems Series

Feverfew
A traditional herbal remedy for migraine
and arthritis
DR STEWART JOHNSON

Fight Your Phobia and Win
DAVID LEWIS

Getting Along with People
DIANNE DOUBTFIRE

Goodbye Backache
DR DAVID IMRIE WITH COLLEEN
DIMSON

Helping Children Cope with Divorce
ROSEMARY WELLS

Helping Children Cope with Grief
ROSEMARY WELLS

How to be a Successful Secretary
SUE DYSON AND STEPHEN HOARE

How to Be Your Own Best Friend
DR PAUL HAUCK

How to Control your Drinking
DRS W. MILLER AND R. MUNOZ

How to Cope with Stress
DR PETER TYRER

**How to Cope with Tinnitus and Hearing
Loss**
DR ROBERT YOUNGSON

How to Cope with Your Child's Allergies
DR PAUL CARSON

How to Cure Your Ulcer
ANNE CHARLISH AND DR BRIAN
GAZZARD

How to Do What You Want to Do
DR PAUL HAUCK

How to Enjoy Your Old Age
DR B. F. SKINNER AND M. E.
VAUGHAN

How to Get Things Done
ALISON HARDINGHAM

How to Improve Your Confidence
DR KENNETH HAMBLY

How to Interview and Be Interviewed
MICHELE BROWN AND GYLES
BRANDRETH

How to Love a Difficult Man
NANCY GOOD

How to Love and be Loved
DR PAUL HAUCK

How to Make Successful Decisions
ALISON HARDINGHAM

How to Move House Successfully
ANNE CHARLISH

How to Pass Your Driving Test
DONALD RIDLAND

How to Say No to Alcohol
KEITH McNEILL

How to Spot Your Child's Potential
CECILE DROUIN AND ALAIN DUBOS

How to Stand up for Yourself
DR PAUL HAUCK

**How to Start a Conversation and Make
Friends**
DON GABOR

How to Stop Feeling Guilty
DR VERNON COLEMAN

How to Stop Smoking
GEORGE TARGET

How to Stop Taking Tranquillisers
DR PETER TYRER

How to Stop Worrying
DR FRANK TALLIS

Hysterectomy
SUZIE HAYMAN

If Your Child is Diabetic
JOANNE ELLIOTT

Jealousy
DR PAUL HAUCK

Learning to Live with Multiple Sclerosis
DR ROBERT POVEY, ROBIN DOWIE
AND GILLIAN PRETT

Overcoming Common Problems Series

Overcoming Common Problems

YOU WANT ME
TO DO *WHAT*?

A guide to persuasive communication

Patrick Forsyth

SHELDON PRESS
LONDON

First published in Great Britain in 1991
Sheldon Press, SPCK, Marylebone Road, London NW1 4DU

British Library Cataloguing in Publication Data
Forsyth, Patrick
   You want me to do what? : a guide to persuasive
communication. – (Overcoming common problems).
   1. Communication. Role of persuasion. Social aspects
   I. Title   II. Series
   302.2

   ISBN 0–85969–624–3

Photoset by Deltatype Ltd, Ellesmere Port, Cheshire
Printed in Great Britain by Courier International Ltd, Tiptree, Essex

'I am not arguing with you –
I am telling you'
James Whistler

'The ability to express an idea is almost
as important as the idea itself'
Bernard Baruch

Contents

Preface

This book is about communication, about particular aspects of communication in fact, especially *persuasive* communication. Now, you almost certainly feel you do not need a book on communication. You communicate all the time. Verbally, in writing, with the family, people at work, whoever – and do so perfectly well, most of the time. Occasionally, however, you will find someone saying 'What do you mean?' in response to something you have said. Sometimes you initiate the correction – 'But I meant . . .' and sometimes too people will say to you 'You want me to do *what*?' Because, in fact, communication is not always as easy as it seems.

It can suffer from being unclear: '. . . you fit the thingy onto that sprocket thing and . . .' (just try it). Or imprecise: '. . . then it's about a mile' (three miles later . . .). It can be so full of jargon that we find ourselves saying manual excavation device, instead of calling a spade a spade. Or it can be gobble-degook. 'Considerable difficulty has been encountered in the selection of optimum materials and experimental methods but this problem is being attacked vigorously and we expect the development phase will proceed at a satisfactory rate.' (We are looking at the handbook and trying to decide what to do.) So much so that the sense is diluted. There are innumerable barriers to communication, not least the assumptions, prejudices and inattention of those on the receiving end.

All this may simply cause a bit of confusion, and take a moment to sort out or it can cause major problems either immediately or later. But there is never more likely to be problems than when there is an intention to get someone to *do* something. Not only has the message got to be particularly clear but, because the days of saying 'do this' to anyone in most contexts have long since gone, communication needs to be *persuasive*.

This book is about persuasive communication. You may still

feel you do not need a book about communication, persuasive or otherwise. Perhaps not, but how about a book that will help you get your own way more certainly, and more often. That will reduce the friction of communication breakdowns at work and at home. Something that will help you to be seen as a clear, authoritative communicator and, as a result, make those with whom you interact follow your lead. Something that will . . . but we are jumping ahead. If you are now prepared to reconsider the question of whether you need such a book, please do so now; and, having considered, buy it.

If I have persuaded you to do that, there is a good chance that the book really will help improve *your* persuasiveness. Think how useful even a small increase in persuasiveness might be to you.

Note   It is said that there are two kinds of people in the world, those who worry that the word 'he' only means men, and those who assume it means men and women where appropriate. I am among the latter, but mean no offence to those in the first category whose fears will not be finally removed until the English language comes up with a new word with the unequivocal meaning he or she. Alas, there is no such word at the time of writing, so this explanation is offered instead.

Acknowledgements

My first job was in publishing, which I joined as a 'management trainee'. One of the things I found myself doing was selling books. A good enough product to sell, but there are tens of thousands of new ones published in the United Kingdom every year, so it is not in fact necessarily the easiest product to sell, particularly in days when no formal training in the ways of doing so effectively were made available.

Only later, having found my way into marketing, marketing consultancy and training did I begin to understand the psychology of making a message persuasive, of selling, in fact. And, in more than twenty years now of working in this field of business, I have been able to develop that understanding further. It is not something any of us will ever understand completely. Indeed because the techniques and persuasion involved must be deployed creatively, flexibly, meeting by meeting, person by person; and because the responses from those with whom we communicate will vary and will always be, to a degree, unpredictable, what there is to understand about it changes constantly.

I am only able to attempt to set out some of what I know at present in the form of this book because of many past experiences upon which I can now draw. Thanks are due therefore particularly to my colleagues in the consultancy field, especially those in Marketing Improvements, where I worked for many years, and those with a training 'bent' from whom I have learnt –and continue to learn – so much. Also to those from many different organizations who have been delegates on the various sales and communication courses I have conducted over the years, and from whose shared experiences I learn so much.

Patrick Forsyth
Touchstone Training & Consultancy
17 Clocktower Mews
Arlington Avenue
LONDON N1 7BB

1

Introduction:
When Things Go Wrong

You probably spend a major part of your time communicating. At home, at work, with friends, colleagues and those you know; and with others you are meeting or talking to for the first time. Such communication will take various forms from ritual pleasantries – 'Good morning', 'Have a nice day' – to deep philosophical discussions. On many occasions, perhaps a surprising number of occasions, there is a persuasive intention in the communication.

If things go well, of course, if you have the desired effect, you hardly think about it. And much of the time it does go well, either because you have a certain inherent ability to persuade or because little persuasion is necessary. When things go wrong, however, perhaps because communication does not occur as you wish, is misunderstood or results either in argument, refusal or inaction –you notice.

Consider the kind of thing that happens. The three case examples that follow, based on real incidents, are typical. They will be referred to again later in the text.

Example one

Ethel Richards is a retired elderly lady living alone. Her neighbour has kindly dropped her off at the shops and she is in an electrical appliance shop selecting a new toaster.

She is a little confused by the profusion of models. She asks the assistant some questions – he is quite helpful – and she makes up her mind. There is one problem, however – she is never very sure of how to put the plug on and would like the assistant to do it for her. After she completes the purchases she asks whether he will do this, but he apologizes and says he is too busy: 'That's not something we have time for'. As other people are by then waiting to be served she makes no fuss and leaves.

- Ethel sees a battle looming, has no stomach for it, or is simply unsure how to go about it in a way that stands a chance of success, and opts to let things lie. A small incident, but one where the outcome may be simply minor annoyance, or downright danger.

Example two

Mark Smith runs the sales office for a medium-sized company. His team take customer enquiries, offer technical advice, handle queries of all kinds and take orders. Recent reorganization has resulted in the merging of two departments. His people now occupy a large office together with the order processing staff, who see to the invoicing and documentation. For the most part all is going smoothly, however the routing of telephone calls has become chaotic. The switchboard, despite having a note explaining who handles customers in which area of the country, is putting two out of three calls through to the wrong person, and the resulting confusion is upsetting staff and customers alike as calls have to be transferred.

Mark carefully drafts and sends a memo to the personnel manager, to whom the switchboard operators report, complaining that the inefficiency of their service is upsetting customers and putting the company at risk of losing orders. He is surprised to find that far from the situation improving, all he gets is a defensive reply listing the total volume of calls with which the hard-pressed switchboard has to cope, quoting other issues as of far more importance at present to the personnel department and suggesting he takes steps to ensure customers ask for the right person.

- Mark intended to prompt action that would improve customer service, he felt he had stated his case clearly and logically, yet all he succeeded in doing was rubbing a colleague up the wrong way. The problem remained.

Example three

Margaret and Robert Hall live in a small close which has a residents' association. This meets regularly and exists to promote common interests, to preserve the immediate environment and living conditions. One of their neighbours has mentioned his intention to purchase a satellite television facility, and Margaret and Robert, who would never consider such a thing themselves, are concerned at the prospect of a forest of dishes disfiguring the appearance of the small close. At the next meeting, once 'Any Other Business' comes up on the agenda, Robert voices his fears, explaining that they will have the unsightly dish now looming over their garden; Margaret agrees, asking the committee to vote to ban all residents from having dishes. There is discussion, argument and conflicting views. Half of those present have not even seen a satellite dish, and with time pressing the chairman suggests they all think about it and the matter is considered, and decided at the next meeting.

Three days later the dish is installed.

- Although they had the best interests of their local community at heart, Margaret and Robert have not achieved their aim. What is more, now the deed is done, they recognize that it is going to be doubly difficult to make progress at the next meeting now a precedent has been set.

In each of the preceding examples basic rules of persuasive communication were broken. In example one, Ethel only had a moment to make her point and get the plug put on. She was not prepared to make her point (perhaps also she did not know how to do so) and the moment passed. Mark, in example two, did think about his communication; he had the customers' best interests at heart, but he only succeeded in having his note read as personal criticism and did not get the action he wanted. In example three, again the intended end result was not achieved, not least because the problem was not perceived clearly by those at the meeting.

You may like to take a moment, at this point, to consider what else might have been done in each case.

The next chapters of the book review some of the basics of communication, the structure involved which keeps it organized and makes sure it relates to the listener, how to plan and conduct it effectively, and some of the specifics of face-to-face, or telephone or written communication and the circumstances in which they are used. We shall return, in Chapter 7, to the examples just reviewed.

Overall the intention is to help you structure, simplify and strengthen what you do so that it is more effective – while remaining acceptable to the other person, or people, involved, whose willing agreement you must secure.

With that in mind we now review the basic principles of communication. As you go through the next chapter you will find paper and pencil useful as there are some brief exercises to do. It is suggested you either resist looking ahead to the answers or, having done so, try them out on a friend of colleague.

2

Communication: The Essentials

The basic objectives

Overall your objectives are simple. Perhaps deceptively simple would be a better way of putting it.

To achieve your purpose you must concentrate on five communication objectives, to get your listeners to:

1. *hear* what you tell them (or to see what you show them);
2. *understand* what they have heard or seen;
3. *agree* with what they have heard (or to disagree while understanding clearly what you have said or shown them);
4. *take action* which accords exactly with your overall objective, and which they find acceptable.

You will only know if you are achieving these objectives if you achieve another most important objective:

5. to receive *feedback* from your listeners.

This is essential if you are to learn:

- whether they have heard what you have said correctly;
- how much of it they have understood or misunderstood;
- to what extent they agree or disagree with you; and
- whether they intend to take the required action, take some other action or do nothing.

Some feedback is, of course, instantaneously noticeable, like 'No' or the dead silence that follows a joke that falls flat. Some may be barely perceptible – a raised eyebrow, for instance, which could mean 'I don't understand', '*What*?' or 'No way'.

All this may sound easy enough, but in fact can present a variety of difficulties. To show you how difficult it is to transfer an identical message from the mind of one person to the mind of another, try the following test. Its objective is to test how well you:

- hear correctly what you are about to hear;
- understand correctly what you have heard;
- agree or disagree with what you have heard;
- act or react to what you have heard.

Consider the following four questions yourself, or try them on a friend or someone in the family.

Question one

Read once and consider very carefully what follows. Then, without lengthy consideration, note down the answer to the question that follows below (or on a piece of paper). Imagine that you are the captain of a ship which is sailing due north in mid-Atlantic at a speed of 12 knots. After steaming at this speed and in this direction for 30 minutes, the captain gives the order to the engine room to alter course through 180 degrees and then maintain the same speed on the new course for one hour. After another hour the captain orders the engine room to change course through 180 degrees back on to the ship's original course of due north, 'to avoid a storm'.

Now write either the answer to the question 'What's the age of the ship's captain?' or 'I don't know'.

Answer

Most people will read this and write down 'I don't know'. More so if you read it out to them. The reason, perhaps – at least in England – is the result of education which seems to foster the habit of paying least attention to what comes first. We do not, by and large, tend to start concentrating until we are into reading a passage. We tend not to listen to the beginnings of sentences, or the beginning of a speech and, most irritatingly, we very frequently do not listen to and get right the name of a stranger to whom we have just been introduced for the first time.

Now this is what probably happened to you if, in answer to the question 'What is the age of the ship's captain?' you wrote down 'I don't know'. Otherwise you would have spotted that '. . . *you* are the captain of a ship . . .' means *you* who are reading, and so the answer is obviously – your own age.

This illustrates quite dramatically that people do not hear correctly what they have just been told. They often do not even listen at all to the first words you say to them.

Question two

Follow the following instructions:

Draw, on a piece of paper, a 2-inch (5 cm) horizontal line. Next write the first and last letters of your first Christian name at each end of the line.

Answer

In answer to the above most people will put the first letter of their name at one end of the line, the last letter at the other, so that Patrick would be represented as P_____K. However, what the instruction *actually* said, if accurately followed, would, for the name Patrick look thus: PK_____PK.

Why do we fail to get this right? It is really quite simple. But the question, as posed, did not sound logical, so your mind translated what you actually read into what seemed to make more sense, and you put down the result, rejecting what you were actually asked to do.

The communication lesson here is an important one. People will *understand* you correctly if you convey to them your ideas in a way that makes sense to them. It is logical for the first letter of your surname to come at the beginning and the last letter to come at the end, isn't it?

Most of the misunderstandings that occur in human communications are due to our failure as communicators to put ourselves in the position of the listener and imagine whether he, she or they will understand what we are about to say.

Question three

What is the answer to the question: $1 + 1 = $?

Answer

Most people, recognizing this as a straightforward arithmetical problem, write down 1 + 1 = 2. Is that what you did? I expect so, like the majority of people. Yet there is at least one alternative answer and there may be a number of others. A designer or artist may see it as an art form so, without hesitation, they will write down 1 + 1 = six straight lines.

This reply may be surprising to you, yet is, in a way, as correct as 1 + 1 = 2. What is the lesson to be learned here? Simply this. Before communicating we should never assume what people should think, or that a statement is so obvious that everyone will agree with it. It is much better to put ourselves in the position of our listeners and ask: 'How will he receive and perceive what I am about to say or show?'

Question four

Again take a piece of paper and write down the first word or phrase (two or three words) which comes into your mind when you hear the phrase 'Paris in the spring'.

Answer

What did you write down in response to the phrase: 'Paris in the spring'? This evocative phrase has produced thousands of different replies in all parts of the world ranging from the predictable, 'flowers', 'music', 'The Seine', 'love', to others with less obvious associations. There is, of course, no correct answer.

This highlights another communication lesson. We should always weigh our words and phrases carefully in case they evoke quite different reactions from the one we intend them to produce.

These four communication exercises illustrate that none of the four objectives you aim to achieve, to get people to:

1. *hear* what you say (or to see what you show them);
2. *understand* what you mean;
3. *agree* with what they have heard;
4. *take action* in accordance with your overall objectives;

are completely straightforward to achieve. Let us find out a little more about what causes these communication barriers, and what we can do about them.

The main problems

The first problem is to recognize that, despite what many people believe, communicating successfully is not easy.

The second problem is to accept that the onus is on the communicator to achieve successful communication, and not on the receiver. In other words if you initiate a communication that breaks down or is misunderstood it is, in all likelihood, your fault.

A number of specific difficulties arise that may hinder or prevent the achievement of each objective:

Objectives		Difficulties
Hear (or see)	1	People cannot concentrate for long periods on the spoken or written word
	2	People pay less attention to what appears unimportant to them
Understand	1	People make assumptions based upon their past experience
	2	Often people do not understand the speaker's jargon
	3	People misunderstand more easily when they hear but do not see
	4	People often draw conclusions before we have finished talking
Agree	1	People are often suspicious of others with an interest in persuading them
	2	People do not like being proved wrong
Act	1	People do not easily change their habits
	2	People fear the results of taking a wrong decision
	3	Many people dislike taking decisions

Feedback
1 Some people deliberately hide their reactions and what they really think
2 Appearances can be deceptive – a nod may not always indicate agreement and understanding, but can mask ignorance or indecision.

These difficulties are common to both the communicator and the listener. Neither we who communicate nor our listeners:

- like to be proved wrong;
- pay attention to what seems unimportant;
- change our habits easily;
- understand other people's jargon.

If we examine the human communications process we can better understand how it works, how failures in communication arise and what we can do to be more effective and successful as communicators. The way we communicate is illustrated in Figure 1.

Messages are received through our senses, of which we have five: sound, sight, feel, smell and taste. We then form impressions and assimilate or associate them with other information and ideas stored in the brain. Before we respond to what has been communicated, the brain reacts in a specific sequence to this new information.

It scans existing memories of past experiences and finds the frame of reference or memory which relates most closely to the new information received. The new information is sent to join the existing memory bank or frame of reference chosen.

If it is associated with what that memory perceived, the new information is analysed and subsequently fitted into the existing memory pattern. As a result of this filing system of the brain, the existing memory may:

- remain the same but stronger;
- change for the better;
- change for the worse.

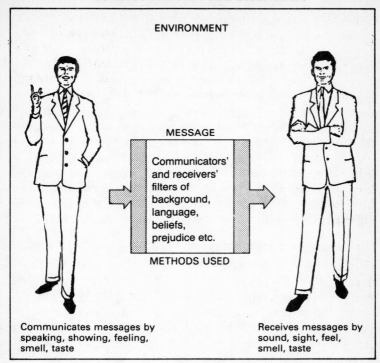

Figure 1 How the human communication system operates

There are constant examples of this memory bank at work. We may call it up in a listener intentionally ('Remember when . . .'), knowing the picture it will paint; or paint a picture that we hope will conjure up the picture we want in the listener ('You know how messy your room gets towards the end of the week . . .').

Apart from reinforcing what we believe, other factors influence the quality of our communications. There are five main elements which, as we have seen from Figure 1, can lead to failures in communication:

1. the value standards of communicator and listener;
2. the message being transmitted;
3. the filters through which the message passes;

11

4. the methods of communication used;
5. the environment in which communication takes place.

These are now considered in turn.

The value standards of the communicator and listener

Our backgrounds, education, beliefs, ethical standards and prejudices all affect the way we communicate with one another. Thus two people looking at the same object or picture or listening to the same story may perceive and react to it in quite different ways. Because of this, it is vital to try to perceive the things you want to say or to show through the eyes and mind of the people to whom you speak. Your knowledge of their ideas and experiences will enable you to communicate successfully.

The message being transmitted

The same words mean different things to different people. Years ago the word 'gay' meant cheerful, full of mirth, exuberantly merry. Today, sadly, it is rarely used in that context but rather as a label for homosexuals. There are distinct differences in the meanings given to words by the Americans and the British. For example for Americans there is no such word as *fortnight*; they say *two weeks*; we speak about holidays, Americans talk about a vacation.

Add to these complexities the jargon that frequently creeps into the language of business and special areas of interest and the result is confusion. As a general rule in speaking, avoid – or at least consider carefully – the use of specialized words – or jargon, because there is a high probability that they will be misunderstood by your listeners.

The filters through which the message passes

Each person tends to think more often about himself than about the people with whom he communicates, and their words, how they express them and the meaning imparted to them reflect this. Yet their own words, prejudices, beliefs and jargon can set up filters which confuse the message sent and received. Even everyday words can confuse or imply different things to different people. What does it mean, for example, to talk about 'older people' – over 60, over 80 or over 20? It depends on your perspective.

The methods of communication

No two individuals hear, see and feel with equal efficiency. You can tell some people something and they understand immediately. Others have to be told, shown and then asked to play back the understanding of what they have heard and seen before a message gets through. For this reason when communicating ideas, you should always involve at least two of the senses through which listeners receive a message. You can not only express ideas verbally, but some at least of them, including those crucial to your argument, can become more firmly established in your listener's mind if given visual representation too (like slides at a lecture). Showing something, pointing or referring to something that can be seen or, failing that, conjuring up a good visual image can therefore help.

The circumstances of the conversation are also important. If your boss is talking to you in the presence of another senior manager, you will not only be taking in the message but wondering how the other person is taking it in too. Similarly if a father is talking to a child and mother is there too.

Making communication more effective

Persuasive communication has something in common with teaching. A good simple definition of teaching (or training) is 'helping people to learn'. Similarly communication is helping people to understand, and persuasive communication is helping people to understand and agree.

Getting the message over is helped by using the classic laws of learning: effect, forward association, belonging and repetition. Consider these in turn.

Effect

A listener will go along with you more willingly and readily if your message shows how they can satisfy some need they already have in mind. Thus the clever politician does not say 'I am standing on a programme of this, that and the other . . .'; he relates to the basic needs of his audience: 'You want jobs to provide money and self respect, you want . . .', and people are quickly nodding with him.

Forward association

People tend to remember things in the order in which they first learned or heard them, especially if the sequence is logical or if constant reference is made to it. If you doubt the truth of this see how much less easily your telephone or car registration number trips off the tongue if you recite it backwards.

This is what the politician is doing when he starts with 'your needs', moves on to what they mean to you and only then discusses how *his* ideas relate. It is what the salesman does when he identifies that you are interested in low cost motoring, that you want to achieve a high mpg (miles per gallon) and only then tells you about 'the model with the five-speed gearbox' which has this effect.

Belonging

People understand more speedily and easily what relates (belongs) to their own experiences, for example, 'an air conditioner is like a refrigerator element with a fan to circulate the cooled air', or 'the plans I am about to describe are like those you make for your annual holidays'.

Repetition

Contrary to what is often thought, constant repetition of a fact, a statement or a warning does result in people learning, as pronouncements about dangerous driving, excessive drinking of alcohol, smoking etc. testify. Repetition is only useful as a means of getting people to learn if used in conjunction with one or more of the three laws already described. A speaker using repetition plus another law might summarize, actually saying 'Let me repeat what I said at the beginning . . .' and restating the same point in different words.

Or to put that another way, if you repeat key things you want to say, perhaps rephrased, perhaps verbatim, people are more likely to get the message.

In other words repetition is a powerful aid to . . . but you get the idea.

Research shows how people forget what they hear (or read)

- 38 per cent in 2 days
- 65 per cent in 8 days
- 75 per cent in 30 days

and some recall disappears very fast. How much of the TV or radio news do you remember ten or twenty minutes after hearing it?

But people tend to remember things which are important or of special interest to them. You can help them remember more by:

- ensuring that your first and last impressions upon them are both favourable and positive;
- starting a communication, if it links back to another, by summarizing what was said at an earlier stage;
- giving them a general idea of a proposition before moving on to points of detail;
- involving them from the start by:
- talking about 'your problems' and 'your requirements' rather than 'what I want';
- obtaining feedback, so that you know how well you are communicating, and thus can judge whether it is necessary to rephrase your remarks or repeat what has been said earlier;
- using more than one sense (for example, speech and sight)
- planning to communicate (of which more later).

Sight, sound . . . and silence

When presented with a proposition to consider, the human mind not only thinks along certain lines, it is affected by what it sees and hears. To a lesser extent the sensations of touch, taste and smell have a bearing on the reception, though sight and sound are of most concern to the listener.

Sight

Sight is concerned with your visual impact as a communicator. This may involve overall appearance. There are people to whom a trained communicator like, say, a policeman will say, 'Excuse me, sir', and others to whom the first words are 'Oi!, you'. Or it may be concerned with detail. Is your expression aggressive, determined or understanding? Are your gestures adding emphasis or implying desperation? (This touches on the whole area of body language, the detail of which is beyond the scope of this book but is covered in a sister volume published by Sheldon Press *Body Language*, by Allan Pease.)

Sound

Sound is also important. Your voice is characterized by the *tone*, which may be blustering, nervous, urgent, desperate or whatever. Also by the *pace* at which you speak. Talk too fast and it can sound glib and insincere, at worst like the archetypal used car salesman. Talk too slowly and you sound unprepared, unsure, or nervous. In addition the *emphasis* is important, the difference between 'You want me to do *what*?' and 'You want *me* to do what?' is significant. Lastly you must consider *inflection*, the change of note that puts, for example, a question mark at the end of the sentence.

Silence

The opposite of this factor, sound, is, of course silence. This is without doubt one of the powerful elements of communication – not what you say but the moments when you stay silent.

The reason this is not naturally used more is that most people find too much of a pause embarrassing. For them, that is. It may be embarrassing for the other party too, but that is less the reason it is not used. This embarrassment is only psychological, and, in any case, the mind exaggerates it. (Try counting ten slowly, or watching the second hand of a clock or watch ticking away. It seems like forever. But it *is* only ten seconds.)

This is important enough to be worth a couple of examples. A simple one first:

Someone approaches a colleague at work. They are busy at their desk. He/she asks a question. 'Have you the file on Sheldon Press?' 'Yes, it's in the file under S'. He points to the cabinet in the corner 'Can you get it for me?'

Silence.

Who gets tired of, or upset by the silence first may influence what happens next. If the person at the desk sees a need for something to happen first, they may either get up and get the file, or say 'Get it yourself', in a way that may prompt irritation or an argument. If he waits longer, his colleague, not wanting either an argument or a long silence, may simply go and get the file first.

Of course, other things altogether may happen, but, if it follows this route, the person at the desk may have to remain silent only three or four seconds longer to avoid interruption.

Secondly, a more pointed use.

A company is considering buying a fax machine. They have had several demonstrations, several quotes and have settled on one as the best buy.

The buyer rings the supplier one more time, and explains that the machine meets their needs, is just what they want in fact . . . but it is a bit expensive. 'Is there anything you can do about the price?' An articulate defence of the price follows, followed by a request to proceed with the deal. The buyer says nothing. The supplier expands on the theme of value for money and ends with another question. Again the buyer says nothing. The second silence is longer, and more awkward. Finally the supplier says 'Would 10 per cent discount get the order?' and, at this stage, having achieved what he wanted without speaking a word, the buyer agrees.

Easy – at least with an inexperienced salesman at the other end – and although it will not always be that easy, it does show the power of silence.

Summary: points to remember

- Unless someone *hears* what you say, there is no communication.

- You do not communicate just words. The whole person that you are comes with them.
- Talk to people in terms of their own experience and they will listen to you.
- When you have difficulties in getting through to people, it is a sign that your own thinking is confused, not theirs.
- When you fail to communicate, it is not your sentences that need straightening out; it is the thoughts behind them.
- Know what your listeners expect to hear and see before you start talking.
- Your communication is always more powerful if it appeals to the *values* and the *aspirations* of listeners.
- If what you plan to say goes against the beliefs, the aspirations, the motivations of others what you say is likely to be resisted or not received at all.
- It is not what is in your mind that matters – it is what percentage comes across, enters the listener's mind and stays there.

Much of what has been said in the last few pages emphasizes that what is important is to consider the listener's point of view, rather than see what you do as simply putting across *your* point of view. In the next chapter we look at this in more detail.

3

Communication: The Structure

The listener's point of view

Your communications will doubtless be with a wide range of people, family, friends, acquaintances, colleagues at work, and others you know less well. All are individuals. All are different. Some will be amenable to you, others antagonistic; some essentially interested, others unconcerned. All, however, have a common view, which will help you persuade them; *they consider and decide on whether to agree to something or not in a similar way*. It was Abraham Lincoln who said, 'When I'm getting ready to reason with a man, I spend one-third of my time thinking about myself and what I am going to say – and two-thirds thinking about him and what he is going to say.' If we understand the process of thinking involved and relate to it in the way we communicate, it will make what we are trying to do easier. While we need to state *our* case and regard it as *our* communication, we will only get our way if people on the receiving end find it acceptable. If they believe we are trying to do something *to* them, to persuade them against their will, agreement will be difficult. If they feel we have their interests in mind, however, it will be easier.

Start by considering the thinking process involved when anyone is considering another's request for action. The process moves through seven stages:

- I am important and I want to be respected.
- Consider my needs.
- How will your ideas help me?
- What are the facts?
- What are the snags?
- What shall I do?
- I approve (or not).

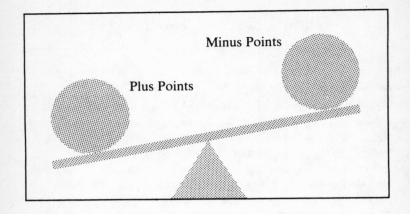

Figure 2 Weighing up the case

This seems like common sense; indeed if you think about it, you will find it is what you do. A good analogy is that of 'weighing-up' the case or argument, putting all the good points on one side, all the less good on the other and assessing the net effect (Figure 2).

Any attempt that responds unsatisfactorily to any of these stages is unlikely to end in agreement. The mind has to be satisfied on each point before moving to the next, and to be successful the persuading sequence must match this decision-making sequence, and run parallel to it.

Table 1 shows the process alongside the persuasive objectives, what you are trying to achieve at each stage, and the technique employed in any communication. The two keys to success are the process of matching the other person's progression and describing, selectively, your case, and discussing it in a way that relates to the circumstances of the other person.

Decision sequence	Persuasion objectives	Persuasion stages
I am important Consider my needs	To create rapport, generate interest or acceptance. To find out about them	1. Opening
What are the facts?	To state a case that will be seen as balanced in favour of action	2. Stating the case
What are the snags?	Preventing or handling negative reactions that may unbalance the argument	3. Handling objections
What shall I do? I approve	Obtain a commitment to action, or to a step in the right direction	4. Injunction to act

Table 1 Decision-making process

When persuasion works, both parties will have gone through this sequence stage by stage. If the attempt to persuade is unsuccessful, it will often be found that:

- the sequence has not taken place at all;
- some stage has been missed out;
- the sequence has been followed too quickly or too slowly; which means the persuader has allowed it to get out of step with the decision process.

Early on, because people need to go through other stages, you may not always be able to aim for a commitment to action, but you must have some other clear objective on which to get a commitment.

21

Imagine, for example, that a secretary wants her boss to buy her a new typewriter. The ultimate objective is for them to say 'yes, buy it' about a particular machine. But it may be a step in the right direction to get them to review some brochures, check the quality of what the present machine produces, have a demonstration, get a quote and so on. Sometimes there are many steps such as this to be gone through before the ultimate objective is achieved. Progressing through each, like steps up a ladder, is significant in reaching the end point, whether it is the top of the ladder or the objective we have set.

Whatever your objective is, however, it is important to know and be able to recognize the various stages ahead. With any individual contact (by telephone or letter as well as face to face), you can identify:

- what stage has been reached in the decision process;
- whether your sequence matches it;
- if not, why not?
- what do you need to do if the sequence does not match;
- has a step been missed?
- are you going too fast?
- should you go back in the sequence?
- can your objectives still be achieved, or were they the wrong objectives?
- how can you help the other person through the rest of the buying process?

Naturally the whole process is not always covered in only one contact between people; several meetings or exchanges may be necessary.

If something complicated is involved, it may well be necessary to have numerous contacts to cover just one of the stages before they are satisfied and both can move on to the next stage. Each contact has a sequence of its own in reaching the objectives, and each contact is a part of an overall sequence aimed at reaching overall objectives.

Although you cannot predict exactly how things will go, anticipating the stages as much as possible, having in mind what you want to do, recognizing when things are getting off track and working consciously with the whole process is very much part of making persuasive communication work.

This does not mean you must adopt a 'scripted' or parrot-like approach, but that you intend, and plan, to control the direction of the conversation towards a specific objective. It helps to think of this graphically (Figure 3), rather as the captain of a sailing ship, proceeding across an open sea and subject to the impact of wind and weather, might take a number of courses, though the clear position of his destination, and imagining the straight line towards it, will allow him to correct and keep on track.

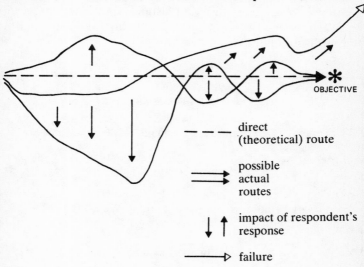

--- direct (theoretical) route

⇒ possible actual routes

↓ ↑ impact of respondent's response

——▷ failure

Figure 3 Structuring and directing the communication towards our objective

Before moving on to look at how the four main stages can be used to make real communication persuasive there are two other issues that must be touched on. Already it should be clear that, if persuasion is to take place, it is necessary to tackle the communication with a clear eye on the listener and his/her point of view. In addition, the whole manner of the approach must be such that it comes over as acceptable, and does not – by seeming overassertive or even aggressive – switch people off. So, the first issue is: *making it acceptable.*

There are two factors that, together, help make your manner acceptable. They are an appropriate blend of 'projection' and 'empathy'. What exactly do these terms mean? 'Projection' is the way we come over to others, and particularly the confidence, credibility and 'clout' with which we come over, or at least appear to come over. 'Empathy' is simply the ability to put yourself in the other person's shoes and see things from their point of view. And not only to see them, but to *be seen to do so*.

It is possible to categorize four distinct types of communicator on an axis of high and low projection, and high and low empathy. This is illustrated in Figure 4 below.

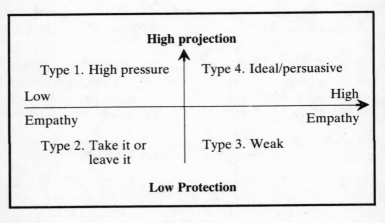

Figure 4

Type 1 The 'high pressure' communicator is overaggressive and insensitive. *They* may feel they win the argument, but in fact their projection without empathy becomes self-defeating and switches people off. The archetypal high-pressure person is the popular image of, say, the double-glazing salesman.

Type 2   The 'take it or leave it' communicator has little interest either in the other person, nor, curiously, his own ideas. A lack of commitment to the whole process tends to let it run into the sand. The archetypal take it or leave it person is the kind of unhelpful shop assistant with whom most of us are all too familiar.

Type 3   The 'weak' communicator is the sort of which it is said, disparagingly, 'they mean well'. And so they do, they have good sensitivity to the other person, come over as essentially nice, but take the side of the listener so much on occasion that persuasion vanishes and they achieve no commitment.

Type 4   The 'ideal' communicator is seen as having a creative understanding of the listener, being well informed and producing both agreement and commitment to the satisfaction of both sides. Being seen to see the other person's point of view is itself crucial.

This is an important balance to achieve. Both elements are important, both can be underdone or overdone. If the combination is right then it will allow you to do what you want, and the other person will find it reasonable and acceptable. Consciousness of such an approach allows you to fine-tune your approach to produce the right overall effect on the listener.

As we shall see, some of the techniques involved, hinted at already in our examination of the structure, are – like the way we ask questions – themselves useful in achieving the right balance.

The second issue is: *making it manageable*.

Like the last section this is something to be borne in mind as you read on. Keep two points in mind; both are returned to in more detail later on.

The first element of manageability concerns quantity. Even the best juggler will fail if he tries to keep too many balls in the air at once, and most often failure means not dropping one ball, but all of them.

The point is well made in a story, which, although it concerns a speech rather than one-to-one communication, is entirely relevant to our case.

In his book *The Past Masters* Sir Harold Macmillan tells of making his maiden speech in the House of Commons. He spent time carefully preparing it and felt it went well and was received with respect. Later he was flattered to be approached by Lloyd George, expressing interest in what he had said, but critical of the way he had done it. He persuaded him to explain. The explanation ran something like this:

> Never say more than one thing. Yours was an essay, a good essay, but with a large number of separate points. Just say one thing; when you are a Minister two things, and when you are a Prime Minister winding up a debate, perhaps three. Remember your own position. There will be few listeners. What you want is that somebody will go to the Smoking Room and say, 'You know Macmillan made a very good speech'. 'What did he say?' someone will ask. It must be easy to give a ready answer – one point. Of course you wrap it up in different ways. You say it over and over again with different emphasis and different illustrations. You say it forcefully, regretfully, even perhaps threateningly; but it is a single clear point. That begins to make your reputation.

He went on to make other points, but the advice to keep it simple, to boil things back to one, or at best two or three points is excellent advice to any communicator, in formal circumstances or not.

This brings us to the second element: preparation. The order and clear thinking that achieves three points instead of an essay, that avoids us finding ourselves going through a catalogue which moves from one '. . . and another thing . . .' to another does not just happen.

Preparation may only mean a few minutes or a few seconds thought, but it must *always* happen. What needs to be thought through, of course, is the detail of the stages that communication goes through, how it will be done, what may happen along the way and so on.

With this in mind we will review the stages – picking up and expanding points now made – and then set out a more detailed approach to the process of preparation that will allow you to go through them effectively.

4

Communication: The Stages

Anything we do, certainly if it requires any degree of skill and particularly if we have to fine-tune what we are doing as we go along, benefits from structure. If we have clearly in mind what we are trying to do first, second and next; how each stage relates to the next, then this element of structure becomes, at least in part, reflex and allows us to concentrate on the detail. We have already identified four main stages of the process of persuasive communication (see Table 1); these are now reviewed in more detail.

Stage one: starting as you mean to go on

Your listeners' attitudes will vary when communication starts, from welcoming to downright hostile. Bearing in mind the sequence of decision-making referred to earlier, there are two important objectives early on:

- to make the other person feel important, and create the right rapport;
- to find out (if it is not clear) what his/her needs may be.

If you think of other social situations, you will realize that there are many ways in which you can make people feel important and become well disposed towards you, such as arriving on time, being properly dressed for the occasion, complimenting your host, bringing a small gift with you, and so on. All these social conventions are intended to oil the wheels of personal relationships, and while everyone recognizes them as such, it does not make them any less useful.

In persuasive situations similar social conventions apply. The main difference is that they have to be much more carefully used because both parties may recognize them as a means to an end rather than an end in itself. As a result the clumsy use of a social convention may be seen as an attempt at manipulation and evoke an adverse reaction. Consequently you have to choose and use these conventions with care. Like other tools they are neutral; it is their use that produces positive or negative effects.

Techniques you can use include the following.

Your general manner

This means your appearance and behaviour. Appearance includes dress and all aspects of your physical appearance from facial expression to finger nails. Make sure your physical appearance and the appearance of anything that will be used – a draft letter, to be discussed with your boss for instance – will be judged differently if it looks really smart, from one crisscrossed with alterations.

Behaviour includes the usual courtesies – for example, in an office context, waiting to be asked to sit down and using the floor for your briefcase rather than the desk – but it also includes such things as being positive rather than hesitant, enthusiastic rather than diffident.

It is unlikely that you will have problems in this area, but remember that your appearance should create a favourable first impression. First impressions last.

Questions and observation

Just as the other person will get an impression of you early in any meeting, so you will want to get an idea of his emotional state. Is he emotionally positive or negative?

One simple way of finding out is to use the normal greeting of 'How are you?', and then really listen to the answer. Is he in a relaxed mood? Has he got enough time to hear your proposals? Is there something else on his mind? Does he want to get down to business straight away or does he want to unwind for a few minutes?

Don't assume that he always wants to indulge in social chitchat or talk business and nothing else. Circumstances will change and you will need to respond accordingly.

Common interests

One way of building a bond with a stranger is to identify a common interest such as hobbies, places visited, last night's TV, today's papers, and so on. In persuasive situations common interests of either a business or a social nature can be used to build rapport with the other person, depending on who they are. The best ones to choose are those which are topical, relevant to both parties, and germane to the topic of discussion. Many focus on the other person rather than you:

> What do you think about. . . ?
> How is . . . going?

In a business context, beware of raising social interests simply for something to say. For example, while it is true that many a business deal has been concluded on the golf course, not everyone plays golf, and not all golfers regard a comprehensive replay of a match as a priority during a business discussion.

Compliments

Most human beings want recognition and association with success, so you can pay the occasional compliment provided that it is *genuine*, not mere flattery, and that it is *specific*, and preferably linked to your relationship with the other person. For example, in an office:

> The atmosphere in the typing pool is so much better since we had that word about scheduling the work flow.

Good turns

Starting proceedings with a good turn may cost little in time or money but set the scene nicely. The loan of a book, a lift to the station, even the offer of a cup of coffee may establish the right rapport before moving on to the real topic of discussion.

Reputation

If you are dealing with someone who does not know you, you may need to establish your credentials in terms of experience ('I have been here for more than ten years'), achievement ('I organized last year's successful meeting'), your understanding of their area of interest or expertise ('I know something about this, because . . .').

There is a danger of getting overly psychological about all this, but used sparingly such techniques can get things off to a good start.

The second element of stage one relates to the other person's needs. While we may know clearly what they are – although there is always a danger in making too many assumptions – sometimes they need to be unearthed. Indeed, whether you discover them accurately and easily can make the difference between an ultimately successful communication and failure.

Making a decision to do something is an action and people act to relieve a felt need. Needs are objectives, goals, ambitions, desires, end results. They are desired effects, not the things that produce them. For example, an engineer wants perfect holes, not precision drills; a householder's objective in the winter is to be comfortable and warm, not necessarily to have a particular kind of central heating system.

Thus, people will only act if they have a need, feel it strongly enough to do something about it, and believe that the suggested method of satisfying it is worth adopting.

They will not act if they do not have a need; have a need but do not feel it; have a need, recognize it, but do not feel it strongly; or have a need, feel it strongly, but are unwilling, for any reason, to act on it.

Different people will take the same action, but for different reasons, for example, foreign holidays. Conversely, different people will take different actions, but for the same reasons, for example to impress the neighbours.

All human decision-making conforms to these basic principles. Sometimes the need is very simple. Sometimes it is intangible, like impressing the neighbours. But always it is an important element in the communication process.

What this means to you is that, from your listener's point of view, he is after satisfying his needs, not adopting your ideas. He only becomes interested in your ideas when he sees how they help him achieve his objectives. Then needs and ideas become mutually compatible.

You can only know how to make your ideas attractive to him when you have identified what his objectives are. When he sees that you are interested in identifying his needs, he becomes much more attracted both to you and to your ideas.

So you need to find out.

By getting the listener to tell you his needs and priorities you protect yourself, interest him much more, and obtain a greater success rate in terms of persuasion. It is essential to distinguish between assumed and stated needs. As you listen to another person's statements you must ask, 'Has he stated a desired effect that he wishes to achieve?' Often the unwary will hear a statement and simply assume the need, but until the desired effect has been stated you have less chance of success.

There are four ways of finding out what is important on the other side of the fence:

1. *Thinking, listening, watching and drawing conclusions*

The point has already been made about not assuming too much, but with care the needs may be clearly perceived.

2. *Asking questions*

This needs to be done carefully, first, in terms of how it is phrased. Ask people 'Are you in favour of smoking while praying?' and most people will say 'No'. Ask 'Are you in favour of praying while smoking?' and most people will say 'Yes'. Yet the question is actually describing the same thing – the two activities being undertaken simultaneously. So phrase what you ask with real precision.

Second, the kind of question itself has a bearing. There are two ways of asking questions. One is to ask what are called open-ended questions, those that do not permit a 'yes' or 'no' answer, for example, 'What will 20 satellite dishes in the close look like?' (see example three, Chapter 1).

The other more dangerous method is to ask a closed or 'yes'/ 'no' question, for example, 'Do you want 20 satellite dishes in the close?' These questions obtain less information, and thus risk you proceeding with a less clear basis of knowledge.

Open-ended questions are preferable for two reasons. First, they allow the other person to develop his own answer rather than putting words into his mouth that he may reject. Second, they encourage him to talk, which at the beginning of a conversation is important. You want a dialogue, not a monologue.

A further technique of questioning must also be borne in mind, particularly in more complex situations. Sometimes questions must probe. You need a sequence of questions to dig for real need orientated information, thus:

- *Background questions* give you basic information from which you can begin to draw conclusions.
- *Problem questions* begin to focus on their situation.
- *Effect questions* help focus on what is happening as a result of the prevailing situation.
- *Need questions* get the person to state needs in their terms.

The sequence that follows, while not exactly representing real life, make the sequence clear:

Where are you?	Up to my neck in the river
Does this pose any problem?	Yes, I can't swim
So what will happen if you stay there?	I shall probably drown
Do you want me to pull you out?	Yes, please

The first answer poses as many questions as it answers – maybe it is a hot day and the person is swimming. The last is entirely specific, and puts the rope salesman on the bank in a powerfully persuasive position!

Without this approach you can be perceived rather as the doctor who takes one look at the patient and immediately prescribes a course of treatment. Most of us *prefer* to be asked a few questions in such a circumstance.

3. *Statement techniques*

When you know the person, or the situation well, perhaps from previous contacts, or if you are just checking interpretation, any statement can have a corresponding question that can lead straight to the moment. As with:

> What will 20 satellite dishes in the close look like?
> 20 satellite dishes all round the close will be very unsightly.

4. *Combined questions and statements*

This can avoid a string of questions sounding like the Spanish inquisition. A statement of fact and a question about conclusions seems to work best:

> 20 satellite dishes in the close will certainly change the look of it. Do you think it will be a problem?

The techniques discussed will go a long way to producing stated needs. Sometimes it is still difficult to prompt change, the status quo has a powerful effect. Challenging their previous decisions can make people defensive.

A way round this is by reference to outside factors, things that are not his fault. These may link to other people's actions, materials, or external forces and are, in effect, saying what was the case was fine in the past, but now some external factor calls for a change.

In example two (see Chapter 1) for instance, the fact of the reorganization may be outside the control of both parties and may prove a useful lever to change: 'Because of the reorganization we must now . . .'.

The last factor to consider, still in what is developing into a complex first stage, is priorities. People may have a need. When they have needs they will have an order of priorities for them. If we know what those priorities are we can refer to them in the way we present our case:

There are many reasons of reconsidering this. . . .
What do you think is most important?

Stage one makes the other person feel important and helps you find out information that will make the rest of the process easier to achieve. The other person is now at the stage of asking 'How will your ideas help me?' and 'What are the facts?'

Stage two: setting out your ideas persuasively

Your task now is to satisfy him on three points, which means that he must find your ideas *attractive*, *convincing* and *understandable*. In addition, you want to be sure that he does find your ideas attractive, convincing and understandable, which means you need confirmatory feedback from him. We shall now review the techniques for doing just that.

As achieving understanding can be regarded as the foundation of the process – it will, after all, be very difficult to persuade someone to a course of action they do not even understand – we will take that first.

Making ideas understandable

To ensure that your ideas have the best possible chance of being enthusiastically received, you need to bear in mind a number of techniques that can improve understanding. These may appear simple but can, nevertheless, have a disproportionate effect, for example:

- *sequence and structure* – these go together, a logical order, a number of points both linked to the way the other person will see the matter and preferably flagged in advance ('Let's look at the thing in terms of methods, costs and timing. Shall we start with methods?')

This helps the listener position in their mind what is coming and is appreciated when it relates to their priorities.

- *visual aids* – these are not always appropriate, but are

sometimes essential. Consider how you would *tell* someone how to tie a necktie. You can show someone, but try telling them; it is difficult if not impossible. So describe, show and illustrate where appropriate.

● *language* – this must be used so that the other person understands; avoid words or phrases that may be misunderstood, for example:

> 'This solution is cheap'
> cheaper than what?
> cheap and, therefore, nasty?
> good value for money?

> 'We offer a 24-hour service'
> available day and night?
> available within 24 hours?
> it takes 24 hours to start and finish?

> 'I will see to that quickly'
> within the hour, the day, the week, the month?

Many words have both literal meanings and other connotations. Make sure the other person interprets your words in the same way that you do.

Making ideas attractive

You will remember that in Chapter 3 we identified a simple fact of human behaviour, namely that people act to relieve a felt need. The stronger the need, the greater the impact of the solution, favourably or unfavourably. Now, by a combination of questions, statements, and careful listening you have either brought the other person to state their needs, or feel you have a clear, factual impression of what they are. At first glance your position and theirs may seem far apart. Consider an everyday sales example: a householder who wants to keep his central heating and hot water costs to a minimum is faced with a man selling a maintenance contract which is the most expensive one on the market. The householder cannot see how his costs can be kept down if he buys the most expensive contract. There is apparently no logical connection between his needs and the salesman's proposal, and he would be a fool to accept it. Or would he?

Supposing the salesman could show that the services and checks carried out under the contract are more comprehensive than other contracts and that over the year the householder will spend less on fuel and will not have to pay for any parts that need replacing. The householder may come to the conclusion that this is the best way of keeping his costs to a minimum. In other words, he can now see how the salesman's proposals will help him keep his costs down.

What the salesman has done is to describe what the customer will get out of the contract, and what the contract will do for him. Put simply, the customer can now see the desirable results, from his point of view, of having the most expensive maintenance contract.

Desirable results from the listener's point of view are called *benefits*. They are what your ideas *will do for your listeners*, not what your ideas are.

People do not buy goods, services, or accept ideas for what they are. They accept them for what they will do for them. Even works of art and antiques are not bought for what they are. They are bought for the satisfaction they give their owners, whether it be visual pleasure, the satisfaction of impressing visitors, or the satisfaction of having an asset that appreciates in value faster than other forms of investment.

Benefits provide the logical link between one person's needs and another's proposals. Benefits are what someone gets out of them, not what you put into them. What is more a benefit may not apply equally, or at all, to everyone. A teenager trying to persuade his father to buy him a motor bike may want a particular model in part because of its performance (a benefit to him), but talk to his parents about its safety features (which produce benefits for them). Benefits may interest people for themselves, for themselves wearing a particular hat – as the company accountant, as chairman of the committee, or for others – their staff, colleagues, or children.

People need to know enough about your ideas to be

persuaded. They do not want, and often simply do not have the time for, a complete catalogue of information about every aspect, large and small, significant or otherwise, of what they are considering. So when you think about your proposals you may well be able to identify many benefits that can be derived from them; but beware of using too many, believing that the more you say, the more attractive your proposals become.

The old saying, 'It's too good to be true' applies here. Too many benefits begin to stretch your listener's credulity.

So, if we have to limit ourselves to one key area upon which persuasion depends (not to exclude others) this is it. People are not persuaded by what something is – called a feature – but by the benefits, what it will do for or means to them.

Let us return to our earlier example of the secretary wanting her boss to buy her a new typewriter. Imagine that she studies brochures on what is available (no mean task these days) and sets out for him everything about one particular model that is her preferred choice.

It is electronic. It has a memory. It has well laid-out controls. It is guaranteed and has a good back-up service facility. It is made by a reliable manufacturer. It has the same typeface style as her existing machine, but more options of bold, italic and other graphic devices.

She puts this impressive list in front of her boss, but he says 'no'. She asks why, and he quotes the price, 'It is a lot of money'.

Why does this happen? Everything she has quoted, along with the price, is a *feature* of the machine. With her understanding of typing the list implies more than it says, but superficially it is unimpressive to the boss; no *benefits* were mentioned.

Undeterred she tries again; this time she says it will:

- allow her to get through 30 per cent more work per hour;
- allow her to present work more smartly and impressively for the customers to whom she writes;
- be low cost to maintain (and will not, like her old one, spend a significant part of its life in bits, being pored over by a puzzled engineer);
- match existing documents, and avoid retyping;

- repeat standard documents (saving her time – but that has been mentioned) which will mean they can go out without his checking, saving *his* time, on a tedious job.

This time he says 'yes'. This time she is talking in his terms, about things he can understand, identify with and sees as important. All the points made are *benefits*.

The presentation of a case can be made more effective by combining benefits in a logical sequence that strengthens the case in the eyes (ears?) of the listener. This principle can also be used to summarize:

This typewriter will improve my productivity, improve the look of the work we send out and impress customers.

Rarely, if ever, are all the possible benefits catalogued. There is insufficient time, some are less important or are not important to the particular listener in question.

Our secretary, on her second attempt above, left out any reference to 'well laid-out controls'. This may be important to *her* but not to her boss. All this is not quite as easy in practice to do as it sounds. It is not always as easy as you think to talk benefits, or rather it is easy to lead with features, perhaps because you can easily infer the benefits they produce, and thus think they speak for themselves.

Let us now link the two elements – benefits and features – closer together, and then consider the precise use of them again.

Making ideas convincing

Remember the listener is weighing up your ideas. He will not just take your word that something is a good idea, in many instances he sees you as having an axe to grind, and may even be suspicious. He wants *proof* that what you say is right. He wants to know *why* that is the case, *how* the effect will be achieved. Of course there are exceptions to this. If your doctor says, 'This treatment will clear the infection in seven days' you will probably not want to know why or how, because you don't need proof. You implicitly accept what he says. Some people build a similar level of confidence with others and can make claims for their recommendations which are never questioned. However, you cannot assume that you can state benefits without ever having to substantiate them. Many to whom you speak will view you as having an axe to grind. Therefore, you need to know in what ways your claims can be upheld.

There are three ways of doing this:

1. Telling people what they have to do and how they have to do it to obtain the benefits ('You can increase my productivity and improve the look of the work we send out and impress customers if you buy this typewriter').
2. Mentioning the features involved ('This machine is much better than the other one *because it is electronic*' (feature)).
3. Quoting examples of what has gone on elsewhere (third party references) ('You will be able to improve my productivity by 30 per cent (benefit) with the new electronic machine. Mr Wellington in Accounts has had one in his department for six months (third party), and has saved the cost by reducing his use of temporary staff' (benefit)).

Features alone are weak. Often you may find this is the bit of an argument that comes to mind most easily, as this is how you see or have learnt about the case. Features used to back up benefits add credibility. Benefits should normally lead, as in (3), but it is possible to state features first using a phrase such as 'which means that . . .' to link the two. There is a danger, however, that an immediate hiatus is introduced, during which the listener is saying to themselves 'So what?', or conjuring up a negative image:

It is an electronic machine – So what
                                 – Sounds complicated, and
                                     expensive

So benefits must predominate the argument.

Two refinements to what has been said so far are worth a

mention. Benefits can be used as simple statements, and also involved in *comparison statements*:

This typewriter should improve my productivity by 30 per cent, the next best will achieve only half this.

Finishing with another benefit produces what is called a *sandwich statement*:

This typewriter should improve my productivity by 30 per cent, the next best will achieve only half this. In addition, what we send out will be more impressive to customers.

Finally, in this section, a word about *third party references* before moving on. These are other people who approve, or have approved, your ideas. They can be powerful persuaders, but you will find them most effective if you follow four simple rules:

1. Use them to support your case, not as arguments in themselves ('For example, so-and-so has found . . .', not: 'You ought to do what so-and-so is doing . . .').
2. When mentioning names, make sure they are people or organizations that your listener respects (supervisor: Fred thinks it's a good idea; manager: In that case, I'll support it).
3. Choose third parties whose circumstances are similar to those facing your listener ('Archbold's in Manchester, who are about your size and similarly organized . . .').
4. Don't simply mention the third party. Tell your listener the benefits that the third party obtained ('. . . Mr Wellington in Accounts has had one in his department for six months, and has saved the cost by reducing his use of temporary staff').

Note that throughout stage two (indeed, to an extent throughout the whole process) there is a need to *obtain feedback*. Persuasive communication is a two-way process. At this stage you will need feedback from the other person showing that he finds your ideas:

● understandable

- attractive
- convincing

or not.

During the opening of the conversation you will have obtained extremely valuable feedback on needs. Now you need feedback on how he sees your ideas meeting his needs, but your enthusiasm to proceed with your case may prevent you from asking for it or recognizing it if it is offered.

By obtaining and using feedback, you can modify the content, method, and pace of your input. The two methods for obtaining feedback are simple and effective: observation and questions.

Observation

Use your eyes and ears to determine his reaction to your proposals.

- Is he using words, expressions, and actions in response that indicate interest and understanding, such as:

    That sounds interesting
    Really
    I see
    Let me make a note of that?

- Is he watching you or gazing out of the window?
- Are his fingers tapping impatiently on his chair?
- Is he beginning to look through his other papers or glancing at the clock?
- Is he leaning forward, obviously paying attention?

Watch and listen. If you are not getting a verbal response and any body language is unclear, stop talking and wait for a comment.

Questions

If you get neither verbal nor other forms of feedback, you can use a range of questions to elicit specific responses, for example:

- to test understanding: 'Have I made it clear how this will work?'
- to check his appreciation of benefits: 'Do you see how this will make the procedures a lot simpler to use?'
- to check his reaction to a feature: 'What do you think of this format?'
- to check that you're still discussing his needs: 'Is cost reduction what you're mainly concerned about?'

His response to these questions will tell you where you are in the decision sequence and guide you accordingly. By asking them you will also keep him involved in the discussion and prevent problems later on.

Let us summarize this important second stage before looking at how to deal with negative reactions. Presenting your case is simple and effective if you follow these basic rules:

1. Structure your presentation around others' needs.
2. Take one point at a time.
3. Tell them what your ideas will do to meet their needs, in other words, talk *benefits*.
4. Show them.
5. Provide proof by means of features, examples, and references to others who approve.
6. Check your progress by obtaining constant feedback.

Stage three: handling objections

However well you have put your case, it would be naive to assume that agreement will now fall into your lap, because the other person will, as part of the buying sequence, automatically consider possible disadvantages in your proposal. It is an instinctive human response to any situation requiring action: 'What are the snags?'

If all has gone well, he may not think of any snags, or objections, and move on to the next stage: 'What shall I do?' If he does think of possible snags, though, you must be prepared for them and be able to answer them to his satisfaction.

So next we examine objection-handling in some detail. First, you will see why objections arise. Second, you will learn how to keep control when this happens. Third, you will learn the particular techniques for handling different types of objection.

Why objections arise

As we have already discovered, people will not normally act without considering the consequences. They may have conflicting needs, such as guests at a dinner party who don't want to offend their host, and therefore keep their jackets on, even if they're very hot and uncomfortable.

But there are other more down-to-earth reasons within your control why objections arise:

- you may not have identified and agreed needs;
- you may have offered your ideas too soon;
- you may have talked features instead of benefits;
- your benefits may have been too general or too numerous;
- you may have failed to obtain or recognize feedback.

Thus, it has to be said that many objections are not inherent in people; they are caused by the way a case is put to them. You will reduce the frequency and intensity of objections by communicating well, but from time to time they will arise.

How to keep control

The first thing to recognize is that most objections have both an *emotional* and *rational* content. Emotionally, people may become defensive or aggressive! Rationally, they require a logical answer to the particular objection that they have raised. To handle them successfully you will need to tackle the emotional and rational aspects separately and sequentially.

The importance of keeping control can be illustrated by the frequency with which current affairs programmes on radio and TV degenerate into slanging matches. If you watch them closely you will see that the trouble starts when one participant says something with which another disagrees. Instead of controlling their emotions and dealing with the point clearly and logically, they criticize each other. The rest you know only too well.

Keeping control is easy if you put yourself in the other person's position when he finds disadvantages in a proposition. If you were him you would want you to listen to your point of view, to consider it, and to acknowledge that your point was reasonable – even before he answered.

You can do the same with objections raised, keep control, and as a result allow him to consider your answer calmly and rationally. In conversation it goes something like this:

The other person identifies a 'snag' and voices his objections:

> I think the electronic machine will be too complicated for our needs and, therefore, it is not money well spent.

You listen; pause; and acknowledge:

> It is a little complicated, of course, compared with what we have at the moment. We have to be sure its better performance makes up for this.

You will notice that you have not yet answered the objection. All you have done is show understanding of the other person's point of view and met the first point in the decision sequence: 'I am important and want to be respected'.

Diagrammatically the situation looks like this (Figure 5):

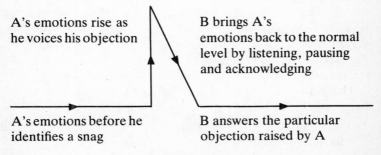

A's emotions rise as he voices his objection

B brings A's emotions back to the normal level by listening, pausing and acknowledging

A's emotions before he identifies a snag

B answers the particular objection raised by A

Figure 5

So often, rational answers to objections are less than successful because the other person is emotionally unable to evaluate them fairly. By listening, pausing and acknowledging you keep other peoples' emotions under control and give your answers the best chance of being accepted.

Whatever the objection there are only three things you can do about it (bearing in mind the weighing-up analogy):

- explain they are mistaken or incorrect and *remove the snag* from the minus side of the balance;
- explain they are overrating the effect of it and *reduce the weight* of the snag on the minus side;
- agree – it is no good trying to persuade them black is white, but rebalance by stressing benefits: 'Yes, the electronic machine *is* more expensive, but it is this kind of machine that allows the productivity improvement I told you about.'

On the other hand objections come in many forms and each may need different tactics.

First, make sure you know what it is you are trying to answer. There is no rule of conversation that says you cannot answer a question with a question; indeed your seeking clarification may well be seen as helpful. A bald question like 'Isn't it very expensive?' may mean anything from 'No' to 'It is beyond our budget', from 'May be' to '*I* can't decide that'. So check before jumping in.

On other occasions you can use a 'suppose test'.

Isn't it very expensive?

If I can show you how the cost can be recouped through additional productivity, would you be interested?

If the objection was genuine the answer may be 'yes'. If it was a false objection he will have to think of another reason for not agreeing and may say, 'Ah, well, there are other things that I'm not too happy about', in which case you can ask what these 'other things' are and deal with them also.

Types of objection

Here we consider the types of objection you may expect, and examples of specific approaches to dealing with them:

Fear objections

Problem. The other person believes that your ideas have unacceptable disadvantages ('I do not think the young copy typist would cope with such a complex machine'). You have to demonstrate that the fear is understandable, but groundless.

Solution. Emphasize elements that will remove the fear – quote examples of similar situations where similar fears have been experienced but did not materialize.

Habit objections

Problem. Acting from habit is convenient because it can be done with little or no thought. People will not change their habits unless they can see real value in doing so ('We have always had simpler machines, I see no reason to change now'). The objective therefore is to give sound reasons from his point of view for reconsidering the situation.

Solution. Emphasize the benefits from your proposal. In severe cases, create dissatisfaction with the other person's present position using the technique described earlier. Then follow with the benefits of your proposal to show that his needs will be better satisfied.

Wrong information objections

Problem. The other person has been misinformed (or misunderstood your explanation) about some aspect of the idea, so therefore needs to be corrected without being made to look stupid ('It won't be compatible with material we already have on disc').

Solution. Save face ('I am sorry if I gave that impression'). It costs nothing to adopt this approach, then as you explain the real situation they will listen without feeling upset.

Detail objections

Problem. The other person appears to accept your proposal in principle but sees problems in implementing it ('I would like to go ahead but it will mean rearranging things a bit as it is a larger machine').

Solution. Check that the objection is genuine ('So if we can rearrange things quickly and simply you'll be happy?') Show him how he can minimize the problems of implementation. Offer to help in removing the obstacles. Give examples of what was done elsewhere to show how the obstacles were easily overcome.

The 'better idea' objection

Problem. The implication is made that something else, perhaps someone else's idea, would be better ('We normally prefer to change all the machines in the office together'), in other words, a change at a later date would be better. Your task is to find out why and deal with the real objection behind the comment. This may be fear, habit or some other category.

Solution. Ask 'Why?' Then, depending on the answer, use the appropriate approach to answer the real point.

Interested party objection

Problem. This may occur where a number of people are involved, and you are perhaps not talking to the right person ('I can't give you an answer without consulting the office manager').

Solution. You have to influence the other person, either directly (ask or volunteer to see them), or indirectly (suggesting what is, in fact, said to them, such as arguments that would appear to be in their interest).

Cost objections

Problem. Here there is no, or insufficient belief that the proposals are worth the money or effort ('It is too expensive', 'It is not worth it').

Solutions. You must establish what is 'value' in the eyes of the other person, so that you can focus on the real need. For instance:

- list (add up) advantages;
- show *total* impact, long-term as well as short-term.

If it is costly of time, money or effort the benefits *must* outweigh the reservation. Actual cost can be reduced in terms of how they are perceived by amortization ('It is only so much *per month*'), or ('It will take only a few minutes *per day*').

Complaints objections

This category of objection is a little different, being a complaint based in the past rather than on the current proposition. Complaints need slightly different handling.

Problem. The other person feels he has suffered, is annoyed, wants action, and expects you to do something about it ('That last report has been with you three days, and still isn't ready').

Solutions. Don't make excuses or blame other people – it only makes them feel worse. Follow this sequence:

1. Apologize.
2. Ask questions to establish whether the complaint is:
   (a) justified;
   (b) unjustified;
   (c) emotional.
3. If justified:
   - apologize again;
   - tell him what you will do about it;
   - offer to do more than the minimum;
   - thank him for bringing it to your attention.
4. If unjustified:
   - apologize again;
   - save his face (he may be in the wrong);
   - explain what he or both of you can do to prevent a recurrence.
5. If emotional:

- apologize;
- save his face;
- wait until he has cooled down.

To summarize, 'What are the snags?' is an instinctive part of the decision-making process. By the time someone reaches this stage he should be sufficiently attracted by your proposal to pass through it without raising objections.

Successful communicators concentrate on objection prevention, not objection cure. Your knowledge, perhaps from previous meetings with the person, may help, or your researches highlight what objections are likely to be raised. As you think about possible objections and how you can either anticipate them or prevent them arising, the following may help your memory and thus your preparation. Using the four arithmetic signs can prompt a useful line of argument:

+ add up the relevant benefits to minimize the advantages;
− spell out the worries one by one that can be subtracted from the person's mind;
÷ divide any snag by reference to the times they will benefit from your idea;
× multiply the benefits by choosing those that will satisfy the needs completely.

By agreement on stated needs and careful selection and presentation of need-related benefits, you can successfully reduce both the number and strength of objections. Successful handling of objections depends on:

- keeping the emotional atmosphere under control;
- identifying the real needs behind the objections;
- using the appropriate technique.

Stage four: injunction to act

You are not always after the ultimate agreement, as was mentioned earlier, you are − or should be − always after agreement to a definite step on the way. In effect you are after achieving:

- your ultimate objective; or
- an interim objective.

In either case, of course, if the other party willingly accepts your suggestions there is no need to actually ask for agreement to act. They are more likely to do so if in your opening you identified, explored, and agreed needs; then, in stating your case you put forward your ideas in an attractive, convincing and understandable way; and if objections were raised you kept control and answered them to the other person's satisfaction.

Attempts to get a commitment without first having created a desire for the proposal will normally be seen as pressure tactics. The bigger the decision, the greater the pressure, and the stronger the resistance. Nobody likes to be pushed to what they see as an inappropriate degree.

Asking for agreement does not *cause* agreement to happen. It merely converts high desire into agreement and low desire into refusal. Even when desire is high, however, a positive commitment may not be volunteered. Similarly, people may want to make a commitment but there are several variations of it, and you want one particular kind.

It is in these situations that your skills have to prompt an injunction to act. In all cases, however, successful communicators recognize that people act to relieve a felt need. They therefore concentrate on the advantages to be gained from a positive decision rather than on the decision itself.

At the stage where the question 'What shall I do?' is being asked you need first to be able to recognize that this stage has been reached – spotting the signals that make it apparent – and second to use different techniques, essentially just different ways of asking the final question, to suit different people and situations appropriately.

Signs of agreement
Sooner or later the person to whom you are speaking will reach

51

the stage of asking himself 'What shall I do?' At the worst he will quickly reject your proposals. If so, you have to identify why and act accordingly. However, he will more often be interested and you will see this interest in his actions or words, signals that include:

- tone of voice, posture, hesitation, nodding;
- questions on details showing acceptance in principle;
- comments expressing positive interest, attraction etc.

These can be converted into agreement, for example:

What is the delivery time on the electronic machine?
Well, if you give the go ahead I can have it in and working for the week after next.

Often when people commit themselves they take a risk. They are not absolutely sure that they are doing the right thing. So you can increase their confidence at this stage by continuing to stress the advantages. Otherwise you simply have to ask. This is actually a stage you can find yourself avoiding. You say things like 'Is there any more I can tell you about this?' or 'Is that all the information you want at this stage?', when you should be saying 'Right, are we agreed' or 'Let's do it'. There can be some embarrassment about asking which leads to this avoidance. You come to the point where there is no more to be said, where the only thing to do is to ask for agreement. The only remaining decision for you concerns the right way to phrase the question.

The following are a number of different approaches.

Direct request

Just ask: 'Shall I place an order for this one?' Our secretary could use this with a boss who likes to make his own decisions. It does run the risk, of course, that he may say 'No' or 'I'll think about it'. If he does respond in this way she must ask 'Why?' or 'What do you want to think about?' so that she can deal with it and close again.

Command

Some people find it difficult to come to a decision or have considerable respect for your judgement and respond better to an instruction than a request ('Let me put the order in today, and we will quickly have every typed sheet going out of the office looking more impressive'). In this case a command is linked to a benefit.

Immediate gain

There will be occasions when, by acting fast, people can obtain an important benefit, whereas delay may cause them severe problems. When this happens you can use an 'immediate gain' to encourage them to take an early decision ('If you let me order it today we will have it to type the Forsyth proposal which must be out by the end of the month').

Alternatives

Sometimes you will realize that there are a number of options, any of which is acceptable to you. By offering these alternatives you give the customer the opportunity to choose his preferred option (for example, 'Shall I order the basic machine or the one with the enhanced memory?')

By alternative we mean a 'yes' or 'yes' question, *not* something which ends '. . . are you going to do this, or not?' and poses a negative alternative.

Third party reference

During your discussions you may find that the other person is particularly impressed or assured by the fact that another organization or individual whom he respects has benefited from your recommendations. If so, you can refer to it as you ask the final question, using any of the other techniques ('We can duplicate Mr Wellington's experience, and improve productivity in this department within a week or two. Shall I place a firm order?')

Summary

If the idea you are putting over is complex, or in comparison with another (or several) is better in some respects, but perhaps not in others, this method is useful. You simply summarize the key issues and link to a question:

> This machine will give us the productivity improvement, improve presentation and will be reliable. Shall I confirm the order?

Assumption

Sometimes things have gone so well that agreement really can be assumed. In this case you can run the conversation on, *as if yes has been said*:

> Fine, once we have dealt with this morning's post I will get on to the supplier and place an order.

This leaves the other person able to agree very simply with a nod or a brief 'yes'.

And that is all there is to it. Each stage, process and technique is simple of itself. If there is a complexity to it, it is in orchestrating it all together. This is helped by preparation, to which we now turn again.

5

Preparing to Communicate

Good ideas, however sound and well argued, however convincing in their own right, must be put over attractively, clearly and persuasively. By now it will doubtless be clear that this does not just happen. The person whom you admire as articulate, whom you think of as having the 'gift of the gab', is in fact normally the one who has thought about it beforehand, who is *prepared* to communicate. Preparation is only a grand word for a bit of thought – engage brain before mouth or writing arm. You only need to think back to the last time you said to yourself 'Why ever did I say that?' to verify that a moment's thought is often what makes the difference between success and failure in communications.

No clever techniques are involved, just avoid jumping in with both feet when you should be thinking about it first. Sometimes this is a second or two, as conversation with someone proceeds. A pause is perfectly possible, just a sentence in response to a question for instance ('Well, I must think about that', 'That's a good point') gives you a second or two for thought. You may surprise yourself with just how much thinking can go on in a second or two, if you do it *consciously*.

On other occasions it needs some real thinking through beforehand. A few notes may help. Or a word with a colleague or friend or both. This kind of formality is more natural perhaps with written communication. If you have an awkward letter to write, draft it – roughly – first. Start with a few words, move to a rough draft, then write the final letter. There is no reason why this cannot, in effect, happen with other kinds of communication too.

Thinking things through

When a meeting with a colleague is looming, even two or three minutes spent quietly with a scrap of paper will help organize your thoughts. You will make it most effective, and quickest, if you go about it systematically. There are, in fact, four sequential stages.

Set your objective

Decide, in other words, what you want to achieve. This may seem simple and clear ('I want the boss to increase my salary'). How you go about achieving it may be more straightforward if the objective itself stands up to some analysis.

Objectives should be SMART – standing for specific, measurable, achievable, realistic and timed. Consider how this applies to the objective stated above in one short sentence. Is it *specific*? Well, yes as far as it goes. But what do you mean by salary? Would inclusion in the annual bonus scheme, an upgraded company car (or a car if you do not have one), or some other addition be acceptable? You need the full picture in mind.

Is it *measurable*? More is, perhaps technically, measurable. £1 added to your annual salary is more. An extra day's wages because it is a leap year is more. What do you mean? Ten per cent more, £1000 more? Define it in your mind, not exactly perhaps, but at least in terms of some definite options.

Is it *achievable*? £10 000 more would be nice, but is it likely, in your wildest dreams, to be agreed? Set your sights – and your specific objective – on something that might be possible.

Is it *realistic*? If 'achievable' means 'can I get this', realistic means 'should I'. How will asking for an unreasonable amount be seen? Will it make you a laughing stock, or mark you down as a trouble-maker? What you ask for needs to be viewed in this broader way to make sure it is realistic.

And how about *timed*? Do you want the increase this month, next month or at the end of the year? After the results for your section are in, or before? How many meetings, or conversations are you prepared to take, over how long a period to achieve your aim: a memo, a meeting, another memo, another meeting, or more?

This kind of thinking, analysis if you will, can pay dividends. It clarifies in *your* mind what you are after and will help ensure that everything that follows is best designed to achieve it.

Do background research

Like planning, this is a grand description for a straightforward task, though one which, on occasions, will take a few minutes. Ask yourself 'What do I need to know, to check, to look up', before embarking on this communication. Staying with the same example, if you want a rise, do you have the record of when you have had increases, and how much they were to hand? Do you know what the trends are in your kind of business for salary levels? What is the organization's policy and salary structure? What is happening with inflation and the economy?

In considering these issues, some overkill may be necessary. In part you are saying what will I *definitely* need at my fingertips for this meeting, in part what *might* I need.

Think through the meeting, particularly the structure

How will you start? How will you state your case? What evidence, examples or illustrations will you use? How will you phrase the final question?

You need to anticipate, but not assume, some of the feeling on the other side. Will your boss be pleased by or hostile to the request? If the latter, what responses will you use? and so on.

Decide what you will need with you

This may seem an obvious statement but it is easy either to leave behind a note, perhaps of a key figure, as you go to the meeting, or be unable to locate it in the bundle of papers you do take. The latter will be seen as indicating someone in a muddle, or less sure of their ground. This stage will include consideration of not just notes but physical objects, a calculator in our running example for instance.

Make no mistake; all this is vital. Good communicators make it look so easy. Silver-tongued and confident, they apparently have no problem getting across what they want and achieving their objectives. This is deceptive. The so-called 'born' communicator, is often simply the person who consciously thinks about what he is doing (perhaps, in part, as the result of some study) and, more specifically, who plans what he is going to do in advance.

It is a process that not only organizes what follows better for the listener, but builds your confidence – and if you are to be persuasive you must have, or appear to have, confidence – because you know it is well organized and can thus work more easily.

6

Communications Method

So far in this book the assumption has been that most communication is verbal and face to face. And indeed it probably is. However, this is not the only way to communicate, and while it raises issues that may be worthy of more separate study, we will now consider the differences imposed by different methodologies. Some of the points made may seem obvious, but the point is – do they make a significant difference to how we need to communicate and the chances of success? In some cases the answer is very much in the affirmative, and the differences necessary should not be underestimated or overlooked. In addition, some of the principles set out here apply equally to face-to-face communication.

On the telephone

Any telephone conversation is simply two-way communication, using a particular medium. It is surely not difficult, after all some people will talk on the phone for hours and hours. On the other hand, like any communication, there may be a good deal hanging on it. Any problem will dilute the chances of success. And the problems of 'voice-only' communication are considerable, and in some cases prohibitive. It pays, therefore, to consider all the factors that can make vocal communication successful.

These are perhaps best reviewed in terms of how you use the telephone itself, your voice and manner, obtaining and using feedback, and planning. The telephone distorts the voice, exaggerating the rate of speech and heightening the tone. You must talk into the mouthpiece in a clear normal voice (if you are a woman, it helps to pitch the voice lower). It is surprising how many things can interfere with the simple process of talking directly into the mouthpiece: smoking; eating; trying to write; holding a file or book open at the correct page and holding the phone; sorting through the correct change in a call box; allowing others in the room to interrupt or allowing a bad quality line to disrupt communication (it is better to phone back) – all so obvious yet so easy to get a little wrong, thus reducing the effectiveness of communication.

Voice and manner

Remember that on the phone you have to rely on your voice and manner in making an impression. None of the other factors of personality are perceptible. Table 2 shows some suggestions to help you.

Speak at a slightly slower rate than usual	Speaking too rapidly makes it easier to be misunderstood and also mistrusted, although speaking too slowly can make the listener impatient or irritated
Smile; use a warm tone of voice	Though a smile cannot be seen, it does change the tone of your voice; make sure you sound pleasant, efficient and, perhaps most important, interested and enthusiastic about the conversation. Enthusiasm is contagious
Get the emphasis right	Make sure that you emphasize the parts of the communication that are important to the listener or for clarity. Only your voice can give the emphasis you want
Ensure clarity	Make sure you are heard, especially with names, numbers etc. It is easy to confuse S's and F's for instance or find 15 per cent taken to mean 50 per cent
Be positive	Have the courage of your convictions; do not say: 'possibly', 'maybe', 'I think' or 'that could be'
Be concise	Ensure a continuous flow of information, but in short sentences, a logical sequence and one thing at a time. Watch for and avoid the wordiness that creeps in when

	we need time to think, such as 'at this moment in time' (now), 'along the lines of' (like)
Avoid jargon	Whether jargon is company (for example, abbreviated description of a department name), industry (for example, technical descriptions of products, processes), or general (for example, phrases like 'I'll see to that immediately' – in five minutes or five hours. 'Give me a moment' – literally?). At least check that the other person understands – he may not risk losing face by admitting you are being too technical for him, and a puzzled look will not be visible. Jargon can too easily become a prop to self-confidence
Be descriptive	Anything that conjures up images in the mind of the listener will stimulate additional response from someone restricted to the single stimulus of voice
Use gestures	Your style will come across differently depending on your position. For example, there may even be certain kinds of call that you can make better standing up rather than sitting down, debt collecting or laying down the law perhaps. (Really! Try it, it works)
Get the right tone	Be friendly without being flippant; be efficient, courteous, whatever is called for
Be natural	Be yourself; avoid adopting a separate, contrived, telephone 'persona'

Table 2   Voice and manner

Your intention is to prompt the other person into action. You should speak naturally in a way that is absolutely clear. Table 3 gives some useful rules.

Be clear	Make sure the message is straightforward and uncluttered by 'padding'; use short words and phrases, avoid jargon
Be natural	Do not behave or project yourself differently
Be positive	Be helpful in tone and emphasis
Be courteous	Always be courteous
Be efficient	Project the right image
Be personal	Use 'I' – say what you will do
Be appreciative	'Thank you' is a good phrase

Table 3 Rules for speaking naturally

Obtaining and using feedback

Table 4 shows some guidelines.

Planning

Because we are attempting to gain agreement or commitment, planning the call is important. This does not mean a lengthy period of preparation, though certain calls may be well worth planning more formally, but it does mean the brain must always start working before the mouth! Making a few notes, or a few moments' thought before dialling, is usually well worthwhile. This kind of planning will help you to:

- overcome tension or nervousness;
- improve your ability to think fast enough;
- prevent sidetracking (or being sidetracked);
- make sure you talk from the listener's point of view;
- assess your own effectiveness.

Talk *with* people, not at them	As a first step to encourage response, form a picture of your listener (or imagine them if you know them) and use this to remove the feeling of talking to a disembodied voice
Remember to listen	Don't talk all the time; you cannot talk and listen simultaneously
Clarify as you proceed	Ask questions, check back as you go along – it may appear impolite to ask later
Take written notes	Note down anything, everything, that might be useful later in the conversation or at subsequent meetings; get the whole picture and avoid the later reaction of being told 'but I said that earlier'; do it as you proceed, not at the end of the call
Maintain a two-way flow	Do not interrupt, let him finish each point – but make sure, if he is talking at some length, that he knows you are listening; say 'Yes', 'That's right' to show you are still there
Concentrate	Shut out distractions, interruptions and 'noises off'; it may be apparent to your listener if you are not concentrating on him – it will appear as lack of interest
Do not overreact	It is easy to jump to conclusions or make assumptions about a person you cannot see – resist this temptation
'Read between the lines'	Do not just listen to what is said but what is meant; make sure you catch any nuance, observe every reaction to what you are saying

Table 4 Guidelines for obtaining and using feedback

and above all it will help you to:

- set clear and specific objectives designed to gain agreement and a commitment from the other person.

Planning is necessary even to cope with incoming calls (at least those that follow a pattern). It is designed to make sure you direct or control the conversation without losing flexibility and reacting to others accurately, without being led on by them. (Remember the sailing ship in Figure 3, it is the same principle that keeps you on track.)

Finally think about when and where you will make key calls – from a motorway call box? – a hotel? If they are important it is worth organizing a timetable of when/where calls can be made. Plan to make difficult calls early and do not put them off – they will not get easier, rather the reverse.

Never think of any call as 'just a phone call'.

How you sound

People considering their effective use of the telephone should know how they sound to a listener at the other end of the line.

This is not difficult to organize; a standard cassette recorder or dictating machine on which you can record your own voice is all that is necessary. The result will be very similar to how someone would hear you on the telephone. Practise simply by talking and playing back. More usefully, rehearse any particularly important, or repeating, call which you know you have to make. Better still, get a friend or colleague to hold a conversation with you so that you hear yourself, on playback, responding to questions and conversation that you were not expecting.

If you have not done this before it is likely that even a few minutes of self-analysis will show you a lot, and allow any specific weaknesses or habits to be improved.

In writing

Letters last. Unlike telephone calls (which are not often recorded) they can be reread and reconsidered. So they need to look neat; think with what trepidation you start reading something that is illegible or untidy. Some may be worth getting typed to ensure the look that is necessary.

No matter what the subject of the letter is, we want to be sure that our letters will (a) command attention, (b) be understood, and (c) be acted upon (it is this that differentiates persuasive communication from simple factual communication). If they are to do this, we have to take some care in preparing them; in this age of dictating machines and rush and pressure, it is too easy to just 'dash them off'.

Preparing persuasive sales letters

Before we even draft a letter we should remember the sequence of persuasion, and in particular remember to see things through the other person's eyes. Then we should ask ourselves five questions:

1. For whom is the letter and its message intended? (This is not always only the person to whom it is addressed.)
2. What are their particular needs?
3. How do our ideas or propositions satisfy those needs – what benefits do they give?
4. What do we want the reader to do when he receives the letter? We must have a clear objective for every letter.
5. How does the reader take this action?

The last two questions are frequently forgotten, but they are very important. It should be perfectly clear in our own minds what we want the recipient to do, and very often this can be put equally clearly to the reader; but having achieved this, we can lose the advantage if lack of information makes it difficult for them to take the action we want.

The most important part of a letter is the first sentence. It will determine whether the rest of the letter is read. People seldom read a letter in the same sequence in which it was written. Their eyes flick from the sender's address to the ending, then to the greeting and the first sentence, skim to the last – and then, if the sender is lucky, back to the first sentence for a more careful reading of the whole letter. So the first sentence is about the only chance we have of 'holding' the reader, and it should arouse immediate interest. But gimmicks should be avoided. They invariably give the reader the impression of being talked down to. So how can we achieve the best opening?

Write out the name of the person to whom you are writing. Seeing it written down will help you visualize his point of view. When possible, always address the letter to a person rather than to 'Dear Sir'. It is much less formal, everyone likes hearing his own name, and unless we write 'personal' on the envelope there is no fear that the letter will lie unanswered in his absence. Keep references short and subject headings to the point – his point.

Make sure the start of the letter will (a) command attention, (b) gain interest, and (c) lead easily into the main text. For example:

- ask a 'Yes' question;
- tell him why you are writing to him particularly;
- tell him why he should read the letter;
- flatter him (carefully);
- tell him what he might lose if he ignores the message;
- give him some 'mind-bending' news (if you have any).

The body of the letter runs straight on from the opening. It must consider the reader's needs or problems from his point of view. It must interest him. It must get the reader nodding in agreement ('Yes, I wish you could help me on that').

Of course we are able to help him. In drafting we write down what we intend for him and of course list the benefits, not features, and in particular benefits which will help him solve that problem and satisfy that need.

We have to anticipate his possible objections to our proposition in order to select our strongest benefits and most convincing answers. If there is a need to counter objections, then we may need to make our letter longer and give proof, such as comment from a third party, that our benefits are genuine. However, remember to keep the letter as short as possible, our aims being to:

- keep the reader's immediate interest;
- keep that interest with the best benefit;
- win him over with a second benefit (or more);
- obtain action at the end.

In drafting we can make a (short) summary of the benefits to him of our proposition. Having decided on what action we are wanting the reader to take, we must be positive about getting it. It is necessary to nudge the reader into action with a decisive final comment or question, just as was advocated in face-to-face contact.

A word about language

Remember our intention is to prompt the reader to action rather than demonstrate our vocabulary (though it is better to be grammatically correct). We should write much as we speak (see Table 3, page 62 for some useful rules).

You may find it will help you examine specific aspects of the language you use in letters (and elsewhere) to review the following list (Table 5).

Avoid trite openings
We respectfully acknowledge receipt of
I have to acknowledge with thanks
Yours of even date to hand
We have pleasure in attaching
Referring to your communication of
The contents of which are noted
This letter is for the purpose of requesting
If we follow the rules for a good opening, we shall also rarely begin
with 'Thank you for your letter of'

Avoid pomposity   *List alternative*
We beg to advise ....
The position with regard to ....
It will be appreciated that ....
It is suggested that the reason ....
The undersigned/writer ....

May we take this opportunity of ....
Allow me to say in this instance ....
Which you claim/state ....
For your information ....
Having regard to the fact that ....
We should point out that ....
Answering in the affirmative/negative ....
We are giving the matter every consideration ....
We are not in a position to ....
The opportunity is taken to mention ....
Despatched under separate cover ....

Avoid coldness and bad psychology   *List alternative*
Advise/inform ....
Desire ....
Learn/note ....
Obtain ....
Regret ....
Trust ....
Your complaint/dissatisfaction ....
Dictated but not read by ....

Avoid cliché endings
Thanking you in advance ....
Assuring you of our best attention at all times, we
remain ....
Regretting our inability to be of service in this
matter ....
Trusting we may be favoured with ....
Awaiting a favourable reply ....
Please do not hesitate to ....

Keep it simple – use short words to the following long   *List alternative*
ones
Additional ....
Alteration ....
Anticipate ....
Appreciable ....
Approximately ....
Assistance ....
Beneficial ....
Considerable ....

COMMUNICATIONS METHOD

Consequently ....
Commencement ....
Cooperation ....
Deficiencies ....
Despatch ....
Discontinue ....
Discussion ....
Duplicate ....
Elucidate ....
Emphasis ....
Encounter ....
Endeavour ....
Envisage ....
Facilitate ....
Finalize ....
Fundamental ....
Generate ....
However ....
Immediately ....
Implementation ....
Initiate ....
Locality ....
Manufacture ....
Materialize ....
Merchandise ....
Necessitates ....
Nevertheless ....
Numerous ....
Objective ....
Obtain ....
Optimum ....
Practically ....
Purchase (verb) ....
Problematical ....
Requirements ....
Sufficient ....
Termination ....
Utilize ....

Use one or two words rather than several　　　　　*List alternative*
According to our records ....
A large majority of ....

A percentage of ....

Along the lines of ....

At a later date ....

At this precise moment in time ....

Due to the fact that ....

Facilities are provided for ....

Generally speaking in this connection ....

I am inclined to the view that ....

In the event that the foregoing ....

In the initial stages ....

In the neighbourhood of ....

In the not too distant future ....

It is not possible to effect delivery ....

On the occasion of ....

Prior to this, we experienced trouble with ....

There can be no doubt about ....

The position will soon be reached that ....

Should the situation arise that we are unable ....

We are prepared to admit ....

We shall not be in a position to ....

With a view to/in order to ....

With regard to ....

With the result that ....

Table 5 Using words

Finally, if you use cables, telex or even fax and have an eye on the cost, be careful of abbreviating too much. There is a story of a journalist, writing a show business features, who cabled Hollywood for information. His message read 'HOW OLD CARY GRANT?'. In due course the reply came back 'OLD CARY GRANT FINE. HOW YOU?'

Throughout the whole process bear in mind exactly with whom you are going to be communicating; in other words, have their characteristics very much in mind.

Is it someone you know well, where a good mutual under-standing exists and you can get straight to the point without too many preliminaries? Is it someone with the same understanding of the topic of discussion as you? In which case no elaborate explanation is necessary. Is it someone senior, older or more important than you, someone who will expect, or appreciate, a little respect? Are they going to be difficult (do we know this or are we assuming it?), and if so do we need to be that much more careful, polite or circumspect? Will they be (rightly) upset by what we want? If so, do we break the news gently or get straight down to it? There are few rules here, but most problems occur not because we cannot handle the situation, but because we have not taken enough time and trouble to think it through and adapt our approach to the circumstances.

There are, however, techniques that will get people on your side, listening and more likely to take notice of you. All involve a respect for the other person and their point of view:

- *Relate something important to people* – take them into your confidence, involve them.
- *Praise as often as possible* – let people feel ideas are their own – and that they are important/worth considering.
- *Give freedom of action* – be open-minded about possible mistakes.
- *Listen to people with sincerity* – show interest in their interests.
- *Create involvement in (major) tasks* – include them in team or group activity.
- *Ask for advice or opinion* – and show respect for their ideas.
- *Give credit* – show up the results of their efforts in front of others.
- *Give them a sense of responsibility* – support them in discussions with others, let them feel they are contributing.
- *Delegate tasks, agree main objectives* – let them work out details.
- *Be courteous to them in all activities* – help in defining problems.

Much of this, of course, comes down to giving some time to work things through, to create a relationship that will be workable, both ways. Because modern life is, for many people, one long rush, communication problems occur simply because insufficient thought went into the process.

7

The Cases Revisited

Now, in the light of all that has been said, let us return to the cases that appeared in the introduction and see how the principles discussed apply to these situations. In each instance, the example is restated to avoid referring back, and then a suggestion, in terms of a more persuasive approach, is made. Bear in mind that there are no 'right' answers, no certainty that a particular approach will guarantee success. The suggestion sets out an approach that appears to be well matched to the circumstances, and therefore would stand a higher chance of success than the original action taken. Let us take them in turn.

Example one

Ethel Richards is a retired elderly lady living alone. Her neighbour has kindly dropped her off at the shops and she is in an electrical appliance shop selecting a new toaster.

She is a little confused by the profusion of models. She asks the assistant some questions – he is quite helpful – she makes up her mind. There is one problem however, she is never very sure of how to put the plug on and would like the assistant to do it for her. After she completes the purchases she asks whether he will do this, but he apologizes and says he is too busy: 'That's not something we have time for'. As other people are by then waiting to be served she makes no fuss and leaves.

This is a prime case of a battle lost before it began. The answer lies largely in preparation. Ethel would have known, if she had thought about it first, that:

● she wanted the plug fitted;
● it might be difficult to achieve this;
● any problems of communication are compounded by lack of time, and in a retail environment the embarrassment of holding up other people.

On the other hand she has time on her side, she can afford to take a moment to get it right, and is in a situation where the prevailing background philosophy of the retailer is 'the customer is always right', and the fact that he is likely to want the business, may help.

So, what could she have done, having thought about it? Her objectives are clear, but she needs the assistant on her side and must introduce the question about the plug at the right moment. Maybe the conversation should have gone more like this:

My toaster has broken and I need to buy a new one, but there are so many to choose from – may I have some expert advice?

This opening is designed to make it clear that a purchase is likely (this is what the retailer is interested in), that it may take a moment (more questions) and that it contains an element of flattery ('*your expert* advice').

Early amongst the questions, 'How hot does the case get?' 'Will this one take cut bread, rather than shop sliced?', she could ask specifically: 'Has this model a plug fitted?' Either this may prompt the response she wants: 'Yes' or: 'No, but I can fit one for you'.

In this case she has what she wants. If not, if he simply says 'No', it should be followed up promptly by: 'I can only buy one with a plug on; I am always worried that it may not be safe if I do it – will you fit it for me?'

This makes it clear that his objective – selling the toaster – will only be met if he agrees. Additionally it may make him feel a responsibility for the safety of his customer – to an extent it plays on his view of her.

Agreement at this stage removes the awkwardness of the moment later when time and other customers may make it more difficult for Ethel to achieve what she wants.

Of course the conversation may not flow exactly like this but it illustrates the simplicity of the matter. All that is necessary is to think ahead, and to approach the matter head on, at the right moment. If the key central question is asked firmly, but pleasantly with a smile perhaps there should be no problem. Indeed it is in the retailer's interest to help.

There is a final option in this example, of course; if she does not get her way she can always go to another shop. Indeed, saying she will do so may be a final way of achieving what she wants if it has not gone her way. Again this would have been difficult in the circumstances first stated in the example where she agreed to buy and then asked about the fitting of the plug.

Example two

Mark Smith runs the sales office for a medium sized company. His team take customer enquiries, offer technical advice, handle queries of all kinds and take orders. Recent reorganization has resulted in the merging of two departments. His people now occupy a large office together with the order processing staff, who see to the invoicing and documentation. For the most part all is going smoothly, however the routing of telephone calls has become chaotic. The switchboard, despite having a note explaining who handles customers in which area of the country, is putting two out of three calls through to the wrong person, and the resulting confusion is upsetting staff and customers alike as calls have to be transferred.

Mark carefully drafts and sends a memo to the Personnel Manager, to whom the switchboard operators report, complaining that the inefficiency of their service is upsetting customers and putting the company at risk of losing orders. He is surprised to find that far from the situation improving, all he gets is a defensive reply listing the total volume of calls with which the hard-pressed switchboard has to cope, quoting other issues as of far more importance at present to the personnel department and suggesting he takes steps to ensure customers ask for the right person.

Here the core of the communication is in writing. The memo Mark sent, though well intentioned, had the wrong effect, and would also have made any follow-up conversation (necessary because the problem had still to be resolved) more difficult.

From the way the example is first stated we can imagine the sort of memo that was sent, probably something along the following lines:

Memorandum

To: Mary Ward, Personnel Manager   3 March

From: Mark Smith, Sales Office Manager

Subject: *Customer Service*

A recent analysis shows that, since the merging of the sales office and order processing departments, two out of three incoming calls are misrouted by the switchboard and have to be transferred.

This wastes time and, more important, is seen by customers as inefficient. As the whole intention of this department is to ensure prompt, efficient service to our customers this is not only a frustration internally, it risks reducing customers' image of the organization and, at worst, losing orders.

I would be grateful if you could have a word with the supervisor and operators on the switchboard to ensure that the situation is rectified before serious damage results.

The problem is certainly identified, the implications of it continuing are spelt out, a solution – briefing of the relevant staff by the personnel manager – is suggested. The intention, as has been said, is good. However, despite a degree of politeness – 'I would be grateful . . .' – the overall tone of the message is easy to read as a criticism. Further, the solution is vague – tell them what exactly? It seems to be leaving a great deal to personnel. Maybe he felt 'It is not my fault, *they* should sort it out'. To an extent this may be true, but you may find you often have to choose between a line which draws attention to such a fact or which sets out to get something done. They are often two different things.

In this case the key objective is to change the action, and to do so quickly before customer relations are damaged. This is more important than having a dig at personnel, and worth taking a moment over. It is, while a matter of overall company concern, something of more immediate concern to the sales office.

So what should Mark have done? To ensure attention, collaboration and action, his memo needed to:

- make the problem clear;
- avoid undue criticism, or turning the matter into an emotive issue;
- spell out a solution;
- make that solution easy and acceptable to those in personnel (including the switchboard operators themselves).

Perhaps with that in mind, his memo should have been more like the following:

Memorandum

To: Mary Ward, Personnel Manager   3 March

From: Mark Smith, Sales Office Manager

Subject: *Customer Service*

The recent merger of the sales office and order processing departments seems to have made some problems for the switchboard.

You will find that I have set out in this note something about what is happening and why, and specific suggestions to put it right. You will see the suggested action is mainly with myself, but I would like to be sure that you approve before proceeding.

The problem

Two out of every three calls coming in are misrouted and have to be transferred. This wastes time both in my department and on the switchboard and is likely to be seen as inefficient by customers. To preserve customer relations, and perhaps ultimately orders, it needs to be sorted out promptly.

The reason

Apart from the sheer volume of calls, always a problem at this time of the year, the main problem is one of information. The switchboard operators have insufficient information to help guide them, and what they do have has been outdated by the

76

departmental merger. Given clear guidance neither they, nor customers, will have any problems.

Action

What I would suggest, therefore, are the following actions.

(a) I have prepared a note (and map) showing which member of staff deals with customers from which geographical area, and would like to make this available for reference on the switchboard.

(b) This might be best introduced at a short briefing and if we could assemble the operators for ten minutes before the board opens one morning I could do that with them and answer any questions.

(c) Longer term, it would be useful if the operators visited our department and saw something of what goes on; we could arrange a rota and do this over a few lunch hours so that it can be fitted in conveniently.

If this seems a practical approach do let me know and I will put matters in hand.

Like example one, this is not set out as the 'right' or guaranteed approach, but it is certainly better. And it is more likely to work because it follows the rules, right back to the seven steps set out in Chapter 3, especially as it:

- lays no blame;
- recognizes that personnel, and the switchboard are important;
- considers their needs, for clear guidance, being able to handle the volume more easily, someone else taking the action;
- anticipates objections, who will do all this, for instance;
- is specific in terms of action, who will do what.

There seems every chance it will have the desired effect. Many situations exhibit similar characteristics. All it needs is a clear, systematic, approach that recognizes the other person's point of view.

Example three

Margaret and Robert Hall live in a small close which has a residents' association. This meets regularly and exists to promote common interests, to preserve the immediate environment and living conditions. One of their neighbours has mentioned his intention to purchase a satellite television facility, and Margaret and Robert, who would never consider such a thing themselves, are concerned at the prospect of a forest of dishes disfiguring the appearance of the small close. At the next meeting, once 'Any Other Business' comes up on the agenda, Robert voices his fears, explaining that they will have the unsightly dish now looming over their garden, Margaret agrees, asking the committee to vote to ban all residents from having dishes. There is discussion, argument and conflicting views. Half those present have not even seen a satellite dish, and with time pressing the chairman suggests they all think about it and the matter is considered, and decided at the next meeting.

Three days later the dish is installed.

This is certainly a potentially emotive issue. It has to be discussed, amongst a number of people, in a short space of time. One at least of those is potentially likely to see the whole thing as 'anti-me'. So it needs careful handling. Maybe Margaret or Robert should speak to one or two other residents before the meeting to ascertain their views. Maybe they could talk to someone, in a different area, who has faced the same problem; and to a TV engineer, so that they understand the technical possibilities for avoiding unsightly installation. All this, and no doubt other things, might help.

What, in any case, are the objectives? To stop all installations? (probably not realistic). To ensure all installations are not unsightly? (yes, but can agreement on that be achieved in the time?) To delay any installations until there is agreement in principle as to how to proceed? (that may be more achievable). Propose a communal dish? (is that technically possible?)

Let us imagine they opt for delay. Then their approach might have been as follows:

- some 'homework' as referred to above;
- once the item is raised to make it clear immediately that they wish to make sure any installation is carried out in the best interests of all residents;
- to set out something of the problem, enough to get agreement that it is important enough to take a moment to consider (a prebriefed ally's agreement will be helpful here);
- a specific suggestion as to action – this much delay – these checks, discussions in the meantime – another meeting (when?) to decide.

Perhaps even the imminent installer would see this as reasonable, and again objectives are achieved.

These three cases are snapshots, typical of so many everyday situations, in business or elsewhere, where persuasive communication is necessary. They do not include every factor that can come up, and what is suggested in the way they are reviewed is not set out to provide the basis for any sort of 'script'. When situations are not stock, but always individual, stock responses are not, in any case, the answer.

What is shown is the way of approaching similar cases, showing something of the techniques that can be deployed, something of the structure that must be followed and the thought and preparation that is necessary. The latter, in the end, boils down to the simple premise 'Ready, aim, fire!'; stated in these terms any other order is clearly less likely to be effective.

8

Afterword: What Next?

A degree of persuasion must therefore form a part of what you do in communication if that communication is to be effective. The question should not be *should* you be persuasive, nor even *can* you be persuasive. There will be occasions on which you do need to be and, as this book has hopefully demonstrated, you certainly can be – provided you bear certain techniques in mind and go about the process in the right way. The question is *how*, exactly, can you deploy a persuasive argument in the right way on each occasion, so that you achieve your aims and yet whoever you are dealing with sees your approach as reasonable and finds it acceptable.

There is no magic formula, so you will not win them all. But, if you work at it, and if, above all, you consciously deploy a carefully chosen way forward meeting by meeting, memo by memo, person by person as the need arises you will win more and lose less.

There may be no one right way, but with a secure foundation of basic theory and psychology from which to work, you will evolve a way that suits you, is respected by those with whom you deal and gives you a good success rate of communications that work.

You may remember that a few years ago Budweiser beer used an old story to illustrate one of their television advertisements. It showed a young lady, intent on a career in show business, saving the fare and flying to New York. She checks into a small hotel and, the following morning, sets out to find the great Mecca of American entertainment. Coming out onto the street she asks a passerby 'Tell me please, how do I get to Carnegie Hall?' Looking her straight in the eye the answer is 'Practise. You gotta practise.'

And that is no bad note on which to end a review of persuasive communication. *You must practise*.

Let us perhaps rephrase that. Do you want to get your own

80

way more certainly, and more often? Do you want to reduce the friction of communication breakdowns at work and at home? Do you want to be seen as a clear, authoritative communicator?

Then bear the principles set out here in mind, and give it a try. It will not go perfectly at first, but it will go better and better, and you will find you can do it and that it *does* work. That makes the practice that is necessary worthwhile.